A MAN WHO WAS
SOMEBODY

MAURICE O'CALLAGHAN

DESTINY

ISBN No 978-0-9549565-1-6

A Destiny Films And Publishing Publication

Published in Ireland in 2007 by Destiny Films And Publishing
18-20 Lower Kilmacud Road, Stillorgan,
County Dublin, Ireland
Tel. 01 2885281, Fax. 012834015
Website. www.destinyfilmsandpublishing.com
Email: info@destinyfilmsandpublishing.com

The right of Maurice O'Callaghan to be identified as the
author of this work has been asserted by him in accordance
with the copyright Designs and Patents Act 1988

A CIP catalogue record for this book is available from the
British Library

Typesetting and Design Artwerk Ltd., Dublin
Printed in Ireland by BetaPrint Ltd, Dublin

CONTENTS

ALSO BY MAURICE O'CALLAGHAN

Fiction

A Day For The Fire And Other Stories

Screenplays

Broken Harvest

The Soldiers of Destiny

The Caress

Films Directed

Broken Harvest

for further information:
info@destinyfilmsandpublishing.com

Website: www.destinyfilmsandmedia.com

ABOUT THE AUTHOR

Maurice O'Callaghan graduated from University College Cork in 1974 and practised law for over 20 years. In 1994 he wrote and directed the international motion picture, *Broken Harvest*. His widely acclaimed short story collection, *A Day For The Fire And Other Stories* was selected as one of the Irish Times Books of the Year in 2005. He lives in Dublin with his wife, Grainne and children, Maud, Harry, Iseult and Suzy. His eldest son, Ed is a top gun pilot in the U.S. Airforce Demonstration Squadron, 'Thunderbirds'. Maurice is at present adapting his screenplay, *The Soldiers of Destiny*, into a historical novel.

Also available from Destiny Films And Publishing

A DAY FOR THE FIRE AND OTHER STORIES
by Maurice O'Callaghan

"O'Callaghan has the true storyteller's gift of attracting the reader's interest and holding it to the last word."
-Eugene McEldowney, Irish Times

"I was reminded of the great William Trevor. This is a vivid evocation of a West Cork childhood."
-Alannah Hopkin, Irish Examiner

"It is a very green Maeve Binchy for men. This is a remarkable book."
-Brian Lynch, Irish Independent

"A remarkable book of great freshness and integrity ... An act of homage to that moveable feast known as West Cork."
-Con Houlihan, Sunday World

"This should be hailed a national masterpiece such is its descriptive power of language and its ravaged beauty."
-Frank Hanover, Irish Times, Books That Made Your Year

"They are beautifully written...and it is the quality of the writing that impresses."
-Tom Widger, Sunday Tribune

for old friends

"Show me a hero and I'll write you a tragedy."
F. Scott Fitzgerald

CHAPTER 1

a man who was somebody

When a man reaches the age of fifty he may well have acquired the skill to hide his deepest secrets from the world but if by then he hasn't lost the ability to fool himself he could be called a fool indeed. Thus mused Bill Cassidy as he stood at an antique mahogany desk in front of a high Georgian window, looking from his mansion onto a sweep of green lawn while he opened an official looking envelope with a silver knife. He had been expecting this because someone had phoned him in advance, but its eventual arrival was no less painful by virtue of its anticipation nor were the contents of the letter that leaped off the page to greet his gaze any less alarming. It was a request, or was it an order, for him to appear before a Government Tribunal on the 23rd March to give evidence at a module into money laundering and the subsequent disposal of criminal assets by various individuals, himself among them. Collusion with various dubious organizations was adverted to, including the Provisional IRA. He read and reread the letter. It threw a wide net, encompassing each and every one of his transactions for the past ten years. It asked him to name and provide details of real estate purchases and sales, bank and credit card accounts both national and international, phone records, even airplane flight tickets. And to name his business associates and dealings with them *"of whatever nature and kind and wheresoever situate…"*

This appeared to be a fishing expedition, a trawl through the names of top-level businessmen like himself who had risen to prominence in recent times and whose notoriety had attracted the attention of some unnamable bureaucrat who liked to wield the axe of power and bring them down a peg.

How had they found his address? He kept a profile lower than most. He liked to think he had ghosted his way to considerable riches by keeping to the back roads and quieter reaches of vulgar commerce but he'd laboured in a line of country obviously not sufficiently remote.

What did they know about him? What buried treasures from another time and place had they uncovered to shake like totems and point accusing fingers in his face? Not many he would wager, maybe none. Certainly none to warrant a hanging. Maybe a mild rebuke. Oh, he hadn't arrived at this station and time in life completely blameless. Far from it. He didn't fool himself. He hoped that age had disabused him of that habit. He knew there were secrets. A man will take his deepest secrets to the grave and those that are uncovered merely mask the other deeper ones. And often the most seemingly innocuous are the most terrible. And his were buried deep.

But he was getting ahead of himself. He'd cross this bridge when he came to it. What day was it today? A Friday in September. He was preparing to head south to drink a purer elixir from the wells around Lough Ine. He wouldn't let this irritant spoil his rest and recreation. This nasty little missive designed to rock his foundations and test his will.

He locked all doors, hearing the slamming echoes resounding through halls and tiled vestibules and when he'd gone the house would stand tenantless and cold except for the visits of the hired help. Maybe the spirits of his younger children, even his younger self would creep out in the moonlight to dance around the fountains once he'd left but his imagination could only guess at the unfolding of such a tableau. Maybe that was a fond and sentimental wish. To reach back to more certain, maybe simpler times before the cracks appeared. Before the ticking time bombs.

Soon the gates of his estate were closing like the gates of Hercules behind him and the lights of Dublin were just beginning to twinkle from Dun Laoghaire and Blackrock around the sweep of Dublin Bay past Sandymount, and out to Clontarf, Sutton and Howth Head. Soon they had dropped behind the silhouetted mountains and the wide, effulgent country stretched before him in the gloaming.

His life operated quite smoothly now for the most part on several different fronts and despite the best efforts of the Tribunal he intended to keep it that way. He'd become an expert at keeping everything ticking over, juggling many balls in the air. He had the knack of compartmentalizing things, everything in its box. He had a tidy mind. He wasn't sure if he'd ever go back to his wife or if she'd want him back. She'd taken the town house in Dublin 4, while he occupied the mock colonial pile on three acres in the upmarket south Dublin suburb of Killiney. His son Daniel was finishing in boarding school this year. His daughter, Barbara already in London, already fled the nest working with some large real estate firm where she hoped to become the equal of Donald Trump. He smiled as he thought of his daughter's feistiness. She had his own spirit of adventure. No one was going to stop her.

And so he rattled around the mansion with its ten foot high corniced ceilings in all seven reception rooms, going from room to room like some enthralled *Jay Gatsby*, admiring its special features which read like a real estate agent's splash of purple prose. This house was real estate nirvana: he still remembered the blurb in the brochure:

Traditional style 'Marvin' Georgian timber framed double glazed windows, underfloor heating in entrance hall, kitchen, utility room and conservatory. Marble fireplaces, attractive covings, centre roses, maple wood floors, TV points, telephone points, ISDN lines, Cat5 cabling, brass light and socket fittings throughout, Bio Cycle drainage unit, jacuzzi baths, superb range of Shaker style fitted cupboards, polished granite worktops, Electrolux eye level oven and grill, Creda four-plate ceramic hobs…"

And so on it read in a blizzard of jargon reminiscent of a dreaded instruction manual almost impossible to unravel. Nevertheless, in a curious way he was satisfied that this house with its grand facade of imposing, bay-leaved Doric columns announced to the world that here lived a man who was somebody. A suitable metaphor he thought was the life-size, bronze stature of Eros in the garden leaping for the stars over manicured lawns, mature trees, rolling hills, a stream, colourful flower beds and the *piece-de-resistance*: a magnificent three-tier cascading stone waterfall with an extensive sun decking area. When he'd first inspected the property a few years before he'd been assured by the auctioneer that for a man wishing to announce his arrival amidst the movers and the shakers of the world, this was a must have. *A sine qua non*. He'd asked her if it was as good as *Gatsby's* place and she nodded enthusiastically without a hint of irony: 'The nightclub? Better, better.' He looked at her again but said nothing except to wonder how her erudition could have stretched to the high level of descriptive competence exhibited in the brochure. Perhaps she merely downloaded everything from the internet.

Not that he made much use of all this space and luxury. Because this was a community where you rarely saw anyone walking, and only saw wandering dogs crossing from distant houses. But never wandering

horses, never ploughshares. Because the once glorious
farmland was swallowed up by luxurious residences for
the discerning, new golf courses, convenient motorways,
monstrous shopping centres. Yet was this not what he
aspired to all his life? Was this not what he always
wanted? Despite its opulence he had to admit to a liking
for escape from its stultifying confines, its nebulous
anonymity. He was escaping now.

His secretary had called from his offices before he left
to give him routine messages: rents were rolling in, a
building contractor had sent an estimate of some repair
work on a city-centre office block; his bank had sent a
loan approval of ten million for some investment condos
in Manhattan. That was reassuring. These days
everything was streamlined, downsized: a minimum staff
of two efficient secretaries who'd been with him for
several years and knew his many moods. Judy, discreet,
competent, self-starting and not too nosy. Madeleine,
elegant, hard-nosed, who sometimes accompanied him
to conferences or meetings with buttoned-down bankers
who invariably loosened up when she walked in by his
side. In this brave new electronic age Bill Cassidy could
now stay cooped up in his gated mansion for weeks on
end, in his pyjamas if he so desired, while his newly-
minted empire buzzed and hummed efficiently and
smoothly like a well oiled machine. Such was the brave
new country, the new economy which he and some of
his generation had inherited and now bestrode with the
world as their oyster. Yet such a far cry, such a distant
country from where he was born, from where he started,

that he sometimes didn't recognize it or himself anymore. He only knew he missed the old days:

"Scant croppings harsh with salt of the sea."

Before she rang off the secretary had mentioned a letter from the Tribunal. She said it was examining some aspects of Bill's business. Yes, he knew, they'd sent a copy to his house as well. That had put a momentary damper on his evening. These letters would probably become routine. He would be put through the mill no doubt by a gaggle of self-important lawyers who were these days examining in minute detail any businessman who put his head above the parapet. Because *schadenfreude* was the currency of the day and lawyers were being paid vast sums to examine real or imagined corruptions while at the same time nicely feathering their own nests with ever more grasping fingers; to such an extent that they had now become an added problem, and the original issue often obfuscated, even forgotten. Bill reassured Judy that he would bat away these tiresome inquisitions with ease but he never quite got used to the sound of his own name being accused of something sinister. He would deal with this when it arrived and it was six months hence.

CHAPTER 2

the saxophones of time

He was a hundred miles from Cashel when he called the first hotel. He called on his mobile from the car. He'd left Dublin late but Cork was a familiar highway. In the heyday of his youth he made that journey more times than he could remember. In battered old Fords and Toyotas with leaking radiators and flat batteries. He travelled there more rarely now. The old ties of father and mother no longer bound. His car was comfortable as well, a Jaguar, and he was taking things for granted. The roads were better too, some nearly gleaming: a motorway all the way past Port Laoise and other previously dull, grey towns now bypassed. It always struck him, how beautiful the countryside, folding away from Kilkenny west to the Silvermines, beckoning and mysterious in the shadowed light of sundown. Yet how ugly the towns you must traverse.

He called Jurys first, his usual stop: 'I'm sorry, sir, we're booked out tonight.'

'Oh.'

He called the Quality Inn, and then the Metropole, each time having to get the number from Eircom, "11811, Joan speaking," or Margaret, or Mary.

'I'm afraid we're full up.'

He tried The Morrison Island, The Kingsley, The Imperial; each time the same story from the receptionist. What was going on?

''Tis the jazz; town is chock-a-block.' That faintly smug inflection that didn't recognize any place outside of Cork as being important.

'Where could you suggest?'

'Nutting in Cork anyway, Fermoy or Michelstown maybe; or Midletin, try Midletin.' The ton in the third syllable became a narrow tin.

So there was no room at the inn, any inn. It was close to midnight when he reached the city by the Lee. Always that old magic feeling when first glimpsed moving up along the riverside from the Dunkathel roundabout. The tide high; large ships like sleeping swans tied up along the quays. On the far bank the outline of the hurling stadium hulking under the yellow Marina lights. The river depths dancing with distorted lights, the river rolling wide and smooth and deep.

There were few cars about. He passed some desultory petrol stations on the Glanmire Road near the skew bridge that arched crookedly over the railroad tracks.

He passed The Silver Springs hotel. He would try one last time. When he walked stiffly to the night porter's

desk he felt his crumpled jacket clinging sweatily to his
back. He was a big man, broad of shoulder with a good
head of greying hair cropped short and well groomed.
His face was youthful, more youthful than his years and
the twinkle in his brown eyes masked hidden sorrows
with which he'd learned to cope.

The Latvian brusquely told him: 'Full up, all hotels in
city full up. Try B and B's out on Western Road, only
chance.'

He heard saxophone music drifting up from Patrick
Street. He could get the faint smell of cigarettes and
stale beer, even from this distance, over the twin rivers.
He wouldn't run the gauntlet of drunks singing and
urinating down side streets, or semi-conscious girls in
high heels and heavy makeup being dragged in
intoxicated stupors to waiting taxis. His own place in
Kinsale was too far. He would go up by Saint Lukes and
Montenotte, to the old city which he once had known.
Old and grand. But that was long ago. Even here things
were changing. Time moves on and changes everything.
He'd kept a flat once on Wellington Road many years
ago in the springtime of his life, in the turbulent torrent
of his twenties. A Victorian with a high ceiling and bay
windows at the front through which the sun shone
weakly from watery skies. At the back it was always dark
because the terrace of houses was built up against a cliff
down the face of which underground springs wept
incessantly. It was cold and dank even on the brightest
summer day. He was careless with his affections and
brought quite a few girls in and out of there in his
youthful arrogance and none ever complained. Perhaps

they forgave him the discomfort in anticipation of an invitation to marry, a wedding band. But there was only one in all his life for him and her name was Eileen McManus, a girl he knew when he was twenty-one: a boy and yet a man. But that was another story and that was many moons ago.

He'd left Cork soon after and made his way along the highways and the byways of the world. He soldiered on and married later and would be called successful in business by any yardstick. Yet somehow it always seemed when one part of his life was ticking over nicely, another part was unravelling. Perhaps that was every man's story. And every woman's too.

There was a mist rising off the river when he eventually found a shabby old mansion high above the railway station to where the sound of shunting engines floated all night long. A lit-up sign hanging on a railing on the street said: "Vacancies." It would have to do. Any port in a storm.

It was one of those ancient houses on Montenotte built like a Tuscan villa with balustrades and arrowhead iron railings, and hanging gardens that seemed suspended high over the river with no apparent support or foundation.

'I've only one room left,' said the sad-looking little man with a wizened face who finally opened the door after a ceaseless knocking, 'maybe you'd like to see it first?' His accent rose and fell like the song of the sea in a sheltered haven.

'It's okay, I'm too tired to be fussy.'

''Tis about to be done over,' said the sad man, 'so I'll

only charge you thirty a night including the breakfast.' He pronounced it 'bruckisht.' 'Was it the one night you wanted?'

'Just the one,' he said, eyeing the threadbare coverlet on the rickety double bed and the peeling wallpaper. There was a smell of paint from the half-painted hall and he'd have to step around a ladder to reach the toilet.

'What name will I put down?' the man asked, again almost embarrassed to ask.

'Cassidy, Bill.'

The man wrote laboriously in a ledger. 'That's alright, Bill,' he said, already more comfortable when he had the name. 'Can I get you anything, cup a' tea maybe?'

'Not tea,' said Bill, 'ah, no, I'm fine.'

'Maybe something a little stronger?' said the man, his eyes brightening knowingly.

'What do you have then?'

'I'm fairly low on whiskey, but gin, or a drop of red wine.'

'I'll try the red, what is it?'

'I have a nice little Syrah, or Shiraz as some of the connoisseurs call it, an old Persian vine.'

'I'll try a glass,' said Bill, reassured by the man's erudition.

The man came back with the bottle of wine on a silver tray. He also left some Edam cheese, a silver knife and some bread.

'That's very civilized,' said Bill.

'A thing a' nothing oul stock,' said the man, 'enjoy it.'

Bill stood up and stepped out into the front garden to

behold, spread out below him, the city of lights and water. The night was still and a white fog was creeping in from the sea. The full harvest moon rode above and mackerel clouds draped slowly across its face, and cleared. There was a smell of night flowers: lilac he thought, and chrysanthemums and faded roses. There were beds of flower names he struggled to remember: azaleas, perhaps or peonies. There were shrubs with pink and red petals, others with red berries he might call camellias or cotoneaster; long forgotten in the hurly-burly of his life. He heard a water fountain and walked to a teak table. He placed the tray on it and poured a glass of wine, hearing its comforting gurgle. He sat on one of the sturdy chairs. The feel of the wood was smooth and comforting and cool against his back. Up here he felt cut off from the frenzy of the party-goers down below. The more cacophonous noises were filtered out and a haunting tune on a trumpet drifted purely in the air. Miles Davis he thought, *Sketches of Spain* maybe. Cork had those entrancing corners that could lull you into feeling you were in a distant, more exotic country. Especially at jazz festival time. The real city seemed remote and his Dublin house seemed far away. Farther away still his wife and children.

He smelled the wine's bouquet and detected a hint of pomegranates. He drank and swirled the wine around his palate. He drank again, this time deeply and cut a slice of cheese. He chewed slowly, savouring the tastes. Soon he was halfway through the bottle and his thoughts drifted to, *The Rubaiyat of Omar Kayam,* a poem that Eileen loved.

"Come fill the cup and in the fire of spring
The winter garment of repentance fling,
The Bird of Time has but a little way to fly,
And Lo! the bird is on the wing."

Time had driven onward fast: thirty years flown in the twinkling of an eye. He drank again and the wine and the fatigue made his eyelids heavy.

He remembered Eileen's face across a dance floor, and the way her dark eyes shone when she smiled. He'd said hello and felt that somewhere they had met before. Her voice carried a musical lilt that could bewitch and it was her voice that he would always first remember ever after. And what a warm and wonderful girl she was, not quite prepared for all the meanness in the world. Her hair was rich and dark and her skin was smooth like honey. Her breasts were full and firm and her hips curved sensuously under a red, strapless summer dress. She had deep, brown eyes that always carried a hint of a smile, high cheekbones and a sculpted jaw line like Ava Gardner.

They met again by the Beamish and Crawford brewery as the setting sun cast a shaft of golden light eastwards along the built-over marshes, alleyways and winding stone stairways of the ancient city. It was the second time they met and he was struck by lightning, and already they were on a train that neither could get off. All in a dream they walked the lanes and quays and avenues of that famed city on the banks of their own lovely Lee. It was the year after *Moondance* came out and that was still their favourite album all year long.

They took up together after that and travelled to many destinations far and near: to the Bay of Angels on the Cote D'Azur and onward to the Ligurian shore. To Paris, London and dear old Dublin town. And out to California the desert and mountains; to the beautiful Pacific shore where high waves came rolling, hissing in six thousand miles from China and Japan.

And should she not have been the one for him? He felt it in his sober heart and there seemed no reason why he'd want another. But the hearts of young men are filled with deep and troubled eddies and their destinies not always in their own control. Inside he wanted to remain but also yearned for a restless farewell.

He left her in one of those summers of the '70's, was it the year of, *The Wild, The Innocent And The E Street Shuffle?* Or was it, *Born To Run?* He left her to follow some distant star that wasn't visible, guided by some compass inside himself that he could not explain, not even to the sky. One day, from the comfort of their Spanish hacienda on a street called Arizona in Santa Monica by the sea, from amongst the banana trees and the bougainvillea he departed for some desert rendezvous, his head filled with romantic dreams and the grand possibilities of the wide highways of America: "*the runaway American dream.*"

He kept in touch with letters for awhile but as time passed the letters became scarce. And she went her way and he went his. She soon came home to the safety of her native city by the Lee. He always said he would return and some day they'd be married and have children of their own, but his promise seemed to echo ever more hollow with each passing year. And that is what she wanted from the moment first she saw him, rearing his proud head across that crowded hall. Loved him steadfast and loved him true, and was prepared to steal away with him from father, mother, far away from home.

When he did return five long years later it was because the fog that strangled cities like London and Los Angeles was in his heart forever, his blood was thinned by Irish rain, he'd always been that water's slave. He came back to find her white face always looking north across the bridge to Sunday's Well, her ears no longer alert for Shandon's bells.

And what good now were tears of regret and recrimination. Too late he realized she was her father's girl and father's girls are faithful to the bone. And why had he ever thought her father's bank book wasn't big enough or that there would be someone somewhere out there to make him happier, to love him better, to keep him from the wilful wind? Why, when he knew that whenever he was making love in the deepest night he was always making love to her? And she he had forsaken. And when he glimpsed her in her coffin clothes and followed that procession to a place below a mountain to the final fields he felt his heart sunder and he knew that it would never be whole again. And if he could cry a river it never would run dry, and so he took to running. Over fields and winding roads he went, never daring to look southward anymore because he surely would be turned to stone if ever he laid eyes on her again.

He awoke from troubled sleep where his head had slumped over the table in the garden because someone touched his cheek. He looked up to find her standing over him smiling the way she first smiled the night he met her. She was wearing a long, white nightdress and her dark, unfurled hair fell along her shoulders. Her face was pale and her dark, her smiling eyes glowed with mysterious fire. Her face in silhouette against the pale moon seemed more beautiful than ever he remembered.

'Bill,' she whispered, 'I've come back.'

'Where have you been my darling Eileen?' he began.

'Shh,' she put her fingers to her lips and said, 'I've been gone but now I'm back, are you glad to see me Bill?'

'Never so glad in all my life.'

'I waited for a long time, Bill, but you were so slow arriving. I could wait no longer.'

He sat up and held her hand.

'Do you remember the evening we first met and made love?' she asked him.

'I do,' he said, 'it was at a bend in the river down on French's Quay.'

'How well you remember.'

'I remember how the sun was going down,' he said, 'behind the spires of the South Cathedral. It lit up your face like an angel's.'

'Can you remember the song you were singing?'

'I was singing, *Going Up The Country Where the Water Tastes Like Wine.*'

'You were a lovely singer, Bill.'

'Not as good as you my love, when you sang, *The Sad-Eyed Lady of the Lowlands.*'

'We walked a lot that evening, side by side, do you remember, Bill?'

'Down past Trinity Church and the sun was all aflame.'

'You said the City Hall was like the Palace of the Doge in Venice.'

'Oh, the things we said and the places that we went.'

'You held my hand when we walked up Camden Quay.'

'And we sat on the high steps of St. Mary's.'

'We looked over at the Coal Quay to the old city.'

'We heard the cries of apple sellers.'

'And guitars playing on Paul Street.'

'And you climbed down to pick me a wild, red rose from a straggling bunch of strays.'

'That bent to kiss the ripples of the water.'

'And I tossed it towards the white swans beating upstream.'

'To the plashy fields of the Mardyke out of sight around the bend.'

'Remember how you loved me that night, Bill?'

He stood and held her hands, touching gently. They both trembled like the petals of the flower garden stirring in the night breeze. Her hair strayed across her eyes and he moved it with his hand. His hand touched her cheek and then her eyes and his fingers drifted downward to her full-lipped mouth. She kissed his fingers and then he seized her in a passion no longer controllable. She laughed a wanton laugh and leaned her head way backward pushing her hips and body close to his. The moon's glow shone across her face and his lips and tongue found her ears, her eyes, her lips. Their hands explored each other up and down in frenzied and volcanic motion. His breath was mingled with her breath, their bodies bound and harnessed to each other, skin gleaming in the cool moon's glance, fingers and limbs intertwining. And their cries of passion flew out loud and high over the city, drowning out the saxophones of time. And flew out loud as trumpets over the lagoons and waterways of light, and over the swollen, silken waters of the Lee. And when the great storm of their love subsided he held her head in the cradle of his arm and kissed her tumbling hair and swore that now or in the future years to come would they ever be parted from each other again.

Into the face of the rising sun he looked and the empty wine bottle stood like a lonely sentry keeping vigil over his night of yearning and of pain. He looked around to find no trace, no ring, no nightdress, no lock of Eileen's hair upon the grass. He stood and on the table he turned down the empty glass.

Pale stars shone down upon him. Red Mars falling, Sirius descended in the southern sky below the constellation of Orion. The morning star, last ghost disappearing before the hunter of the east. The full moon still hung in the northwest over Blarney, Mushera, the Ballyhoura Hills. Cork was rising in the flooding brightness of the equinoxal sun and the tide that flooded up the harbour late last night had long since ebbed from inlets and from estuaries out along the harbour. Down the mighty river ships were slouching out into the main channel bound for Valparaiso and places far away, while the ferry at Ringaskiddy, come west from Swansea was disgorging its load of weary travellers. Across in Cobh the cathedral

belfry was lassoed in a noose of blood-red light. Jack
Doyle, the Gorgeous Gael, had started here, from here
the Titanic sailed. Before her the Jeanie Johnston: coffin
ship crossing the Atlantic with poor lost Famine souls.
From here he first set sail himself in the careless
squandering of his youth. Bill Cassidy gone off to
conquer the world with a jaunty cigarette between his
teeth. Out in the hissing, quaking estuaries, flocks of
seabirds were awake in search of sustenance before their
winter migrations: sooty shearwaters, divers and
feathered waders, egrets and spoonbills; lone herons
trundling into flight with craking calls. The morning was
luminous, still, pristine, smelling of fish and seaweed.

He'd left his lodgings and driven past the sleeping
rows of cottages, past the dregs of last night's carousing
in the winding city streets, a city that always surprised
him with its watery face. Water everywhere, flowing
under broken bridges, past green and slippy concrete
steps centuries old, constructed when Cork really was
the shabby Venice of the western world as depicted in
the painting that hung in the Crawford Gallery; when
boats and boatmen tied up in the switchback channels
of what was now St. Patrick Street and the Grand
Parade. Before the marshes and the waterways were
filled in, when sailors with strange garb in sailing ships
from far-flung lands haunted the crooked streets and
warehouse taverns, searching for some shelter from the
tempest, a love to call their own. And some traces of
these foreign traders had remained, these Levantine and
Latin wanderers: in the strange, sing-song lilt of the
accents, in the pinched and bitter faces of the poor, in

the bursts of wit and wisdom and sudden anger, and often in their warm and generous hearts. For this was a city rooted in the past and never really could be modern. Too eccentric, too haphazard. A city of Lavitt's Quays and Lapp's Quays and Queen's Old Castles; where the subterranean waters were never far below; where to build permanently always imposed a risk, where houses and churches leant at curious angles and chimneys toppled over in the night. And love too was a game of chance.

Today the dream of last night would not leave his head and its haunting would remain for many days to come. By late afternoon he was ready to head west. He'd attended to business. The staff at his swanky hotel in Kinsale had shown suitable deference when he'd walked in. They rarely saw him but with the instinctive intuition people have for recognizing the man who pulled the strings they jumped to extra eager attention, the prettier ones making every effort to catch his eye, to smile, to bask in the aura of the top dog's reflected power. A particularly attractive and personable young lady who told him her name was Corinne registered on his consciousness momentarily before the exigencies of business reasserted their urgent call. But he did feel a sense of reassurance that such a person worked for him in the public relations department. He should note her down for future promotion he thought.

He quickly ran through financial details with his managers, Brian Bracken, the principal and Laurence O'Grady the assistant. He made a mental note to take everything they said with an extra leavening of salt.

He'd been around too long, he was too wary to take everything as presented at face value. He would always manage the managers. Bracken was capable, diligent, well organized, but didn't always look you in the eye. Didn't reveal his entire hand. There was something about his long, thin face, his bright, red hair and the way his brows knit in worried agitation whenever an unexpected question was posited that suggested to Bill that this very tall, thin man, (six foot four at least) was not one hundred per cent trustworthy. And yet he had a kind of vulnerable sorrow about him that women seemed to like. The female staff worked very well for him and Bill noticed his easy relationship with Corinne Daly, the girl who'd caught his eye. Perhaps his single status made him a potential catch, particularly given the rumour of his amorous prowess although he was unusually discreet in the manifestation of such matters. Yon Cassius had a lean and hungry look and perhaps thought too much.

O'Grady on the other hand was gregarious, confident, sometimes overly familiar, with edges to be smoothed. That was alright. With his thick, curling blonde hair, powerful rugby hooker build and luminous blue eyes he was a good front-of-house man. Besides he was happily married with one or was it two children which suggested solidity and dependability. Perhaps sophistication would come in time. Bill hadn't yet made up his mind which one to have with him on the inside track. But he had an uncanny nose for sniffing which way the wind was blowing; any sudden shifts in attitude, in the temperature with which he was greeted on his monthly visits registered immediately. Or so he thought. At the moment they did the job he required them for. Bracken was maybe fifteen years younger than himself. O'Grady maybe twenty. That considerable gap of years meant that they were unlikely to catch him. They were like three trains going in the one direction at the same speed, only he had left the station well ahead of them.

Later he drove to his stud farm near Carrigaline and had a cup of tea with Monica who looked after the mares and foals. She promised a decent Cheltenham entry one of these days but he was aware that this was more a fond hope than a definite prospect. But he loved horses, although his father could never afford anything in the old days, except Irish draughts, the faithful, unglamorous journeymen horses of his youth. Maybe he'd have more luck with the Belmont Park Syndicate in New York. He bought the stud farm when the previous owner, a sporting life solicitor had died of a sudden heart attack and his widow wanted to offload it to pay the bills. Monica came with it. She was from Germany but had lived in Ireland for many years. She brought a brisk, Aryan efficiency to the running of the farm. He made nothing from racing but the sale of the foals at least paid for the running costs. Monica ran the place like clockwork with a small staff. He rarely interfered, but sometimes brought some businessman or other there that he wanted to impress. They'd ride out on Sunday mornings, have lunch, fly back from the nearby airport. It served a useful purpose.

He drove out into the gathering twilight over new roads that were boreens when first he started roaming in the late sixties. Familiar landmarks now surrounded with new housing estates, new roundabouts, flyovers, bypasses, cranes on the skyline. Bishopstown, the Viaduct, onwards to Crossbarry where his father fought for Ireland more than eighty years before. And who was Tom Cassidy now they'd never know?

And he, Bill, Tom's son? What would they make of him? All he knew was that time was running faster every year. Fifty-three next birthday and each day harder to face. More aches more fears despite his wealth. He still kept his lean, taut figure but closer inspection revealed irreversible lines around his eyes and the inevitable graying of his once abundant, curling, black locks. Once he had energy to burn, but now he was sometimes tired, often worried, though on the surface he seemed the acme of success. Had he not reached his dream? He had money and power, yet other men were still wealthier, more powerful. In his youth he had no money but a sense of reckless possibilities carried him onward. Old friends fell by the wayside and still he rode the waves. He missed his great and wasted mentor, Wild Frank Russell, who always laughed at life, who scorned wealth and who soldiered with him through hard times and through good, on and off for twenty-five years. But Wild Frank had gone out like a light one winter's evening on a train to London and never woke up. Never knew what hit him. The ambulance medics who found him said it was the heart. Wild Frank was a soldier, a scholar, a harum- scarum, happy go lucky, wild and crazy desperado waiting for a train. He died young, forever young at heart, only sixty-five, and he would never moulder in some ward for the sick and indigent.

When Bill went out west, which was rarely now he was thought of as a big shot: they'd seen him in the papers, read of his exploits. Would the reality stand up to a forensic examination? Another old acquaintance with whom he kept a link, a line directly back to the certainties of youth, and whom he hoped to bump into between the hills and sea, didn't seem to think so. He hadn't seen him for a good few years. The man who was his conscience, his anchorite, his doleful prophet crying in the wilderness. He shouldn't be too hard to find, the redoubtable Joey Harrison.

CHAPTER 3

dark birds of shame

He followed the sinking sun. Felt himself sinking back to
earlier days, other times, the further on he travelled. High
ridges to the south obscured vistas of the sea, suddenly
glimpsed between indentations and devil's bits of land:
the intense blue seas of childhood that first unfolded
before his eyes as he cycled out by Inchydoney and the
Virgin Mary's banks. Where his old schoolmate Willie
John died, pulled under by a roiling, rogue wave, the
bellowing wave of Cliona. The land was undulating.
Those green ridges like a bulwark on the southern horizon
kept back that mythical wave, and then the land rolled,
curved in multicoloured patterns: deep green of grass,
gold of wheat and barley stubble, lighter green leaves of
sugar beet, yellow of rapeseed, from where the narrow
Arigideen river ran east under Corrin Hill to Timoleague.
And from there the land swept downward to broader
fields where cattle and horses grazed in the wide flood

plains of another bigger river, the Bandon, as it made its final majestic progress to Kinsale. The further on he went the more muscular the landscape became. Higher to the north the land rose to the heights of the Caha Mountains: the rearing, proud peaks of Owen, Sheha, Douce and Douchaill. Ever westward as the land became rougher, more jagged: twisting, slashing rocks ground out into fantastic shapes aeons ago. Sheep clung to high strips of pasture between the rocks, solitary hooded crows and ravens flew to empty nests; clusters of starlings swooped in ever changing patterns against the setting sun's rays. Peregrines hovered on drafts of rising air, ospreys coming in from the sea cliffs bespoke stormy weather.

He stopped in the town where he went to school in the shadow of the mountains. Where he hoped things hadn't changed too much, where on the off-chance someone might still know him and time might have been turning somewhat slower. He drove into the backyard of a public house and parked his Jag. Some little boys nosed curiously against its windows as he entered the bar. It was a dark, cavernous place with a patterned carpet and imitation maple on the floor. Garish banners advertising beer hung like a clothesline across the muddy-brown ceiling. There was a pop song playing on an invisible radio coming from several large loudspeakers and the walls were adorned with pictures that signified a promised land of beaches, golf courses, charming coves with sailing ships, the good life, smoked salmon sandwiches, prawn cocktails, horse riding: that read:

"West Cork, a place apart."

The one picture he liked was of a Cork hurler wielding
a *camán*, the ancient, fierce, balletic game he played
when first he grew a man. It was about seven o'clock on
this late September evening and the place was empty as
a grave. The gloomy interior filled him with foreboding.
The charm of the old country pub that he remembered
had vanished and the skeletal remains grinned back at
him, mocking his memories. The owner came in and Bill
vaguely recognized him from somewhere in the past. He
wasn't sure if he was recognized in turn. The man was
tall and straight with hair turning grey and he'd retained
a certain youthful innocence about his face. But the eyes
were wary of strangers.

'How are you?' he asked Bill without enthusiasm.

'Oh, pretty good,' said Bill, trying to be cheerful.

'What can I get you?'

'Give me a Guinness.'

'A pint?'

'A pint is fine.'

Bill pulled over a tall stool and sat on it. He looked
idly around. There was a wintry chill to the place and no
fire lighting. There was a vague smell of stale beer and
cold cooking. The owner washed a few glasses and then
fiddled with the radio dial. A young disc jockey with an
accent that was trying to be mid-Atlantic with a Cork
brogue clutching at its edges announced the name of the
pop song just finished.

'What station is that?' asked Bill.

'County Sound,' said the owner.

'A Dublin station?'

'Not at all,' said the owner, 'that's a Cork station, and

a West Cork station at that. We have all our own stuff around here now: satellite television, internet broadband, flat screens, you name it.'

The speech was broad, rich, confident not ashamed of its origins. Lots of rolling r's and sibilant s's. There was a soccer match playing on the huge plasma screen on the wall. The sound was turned down but he recognized Manchester United. 'Things have come a long way,' said Bill.

'Yerra what,' said the owner. The phrase was a throwaway, denoting something axiomatic, a given: a universe of progress, of achievement, of modernity. Silence again. The deejay was talking about upcoming events, a concert by Westlife, Bruce Springsteen the following week. It was all happening.

He became aware of someone scrutinizing him in detail. He stole a half-glance at another customer who had slipped in unnoticed in the gloom and who was leaning on the counter. A pair of critical brown eyes, a half curled lip, a sour visage greeted his smile: 'Good weather...Jesus, Joey...I didn't see you there.'

Joey continued to stare at him and said nothing. The ghost of a smile twisted his lips, positive or negative Bill couldn't tell. Then Joey said suddenly, 'You haven't changed a bit.'

'Huh,' said Bill aware of the irony.

He rose and took his newly filled pint around the counter and placed it beside Joey. Then he stretched out his hand which Joey took slowly. Bill pumped his hand and slapped Joey on the back. 'Jesus, how long has it been?..five years, I don't know...'

'You're still the same oul smoocher,' said Joey and suddenly began to cackle with hoarse laughter that ended in a spluttering, hacking cough. Bill was nonplussed. His old friend's once handsome face, a face like Robert De Niro's with the same hooded, smiling eyes, the same curling lips, the strong, noble Roman nose, had become somewhat raddled, pockmarked, puffed, like a map of broken dreams.

Bill stood back from him in genuine affection and looked him up and down. 'Well, Joey Harrison how the hell are you, you old son of a gun?'

Joey thought a minute and then said with a poker face: 'Not bad, could be worse I suppose.'

'Well things are very good around here by all accounts,' said Bill.

'By all accounts,' said Joey with sarcasm and took a slug of his pint.

'Never better,' said the barman, eager not to let the side down.

'You know this man of course,' said Joey, indicating the barman.

'His face is familiar,' said Bill, diplomatically, 'but I couldn't put a name on him to save my life.'

'How d'you mean familiar?' said Joey, 'wasn't he only a few classes behind you in school, with Master Kelly, the hard bastard.'

'Ah, more than that,' said the barman, 'six or seven I'd say. You fellas were finishing when I was only starting.'

Bill stared into the crystal ball of the past: national school and Master Kelly were a thousand light years ago, across time and space, oceans and crowded cities, and a hundred false dawns and disappointments; the crystal long since grown opaque. He shook his head and gave up.

'Jim Keohane,' said the barman stretching out his hand.

'Jim Keohane,' said Bill, 'I wouldn't know you from a ton of bricks. I'm Bill Cassidy.'

'Oh, now, I had a fair idea who you were alright.' said Keohane.

'Christ, but you're some bollocks,' said Joey, half mocking, and leant back to take an eyeful of Bill's elegant attire: neat navy jacket, pressed trousers, expensive black shiny shoes with tassels and slim soles.

Bill again tried to bridge the gulf of years and disentangle the twisted whorls of fate that had sent them spinning out like stars in an expanding universe away from the sad old town, the rushing river from the mountains, the green foothills looking out over the sea and the rugged fields of home. But like ships with tattered sails they seemed to have passed too far beyond each other's hail. They both were grasping for a foothold, some common ground to regain.

'Fill another pint for that man,' said Joey trying to organize his thoughts. Keohane drew down another glass and Bill and Joey sat captive in the gloom and wondered what to say next. When the storm of the porter had subsided in the glass Keohane said: 'You two go back a bit.'

'Back a bit is right,' said Joey

'Thirty-five years I suppose,' said Bill, 'on and off.'

'We did a lot of mad things in our younger days right enough,' said Joey, 'but those days are gone. This man is in a different league nowadays. We couldn't keep up with him...ah yes, the light of other days.'

'There's been a few changes around here since you boys were on the ran tan,' said Keohane.

'Changes is it?' asked Joey, 'sure we're like strangers in our own place nowadays, what with every kind of bloody foreigner taking over. I wouldn't know half the people coming into this pub on any given night of the week.'

'That's progress for you,' said Keohane nodding sagely.

'Progress my ass,' snorted Joey, 'you might call it that, more customers for you. I'd have another word for it.'

'But what can we do about it?' asked Keohane with a kind of plaintive, resigned look on his face.'

'We can do plenty,' said Joey, 'we can shut the borders first of all and secondly, there's still a few lads around who haven't sold out, who can still deal the cards, if you understand me.' And he winked knowingly at Bill and drank and brooded into his glass. Bill changed the subject.

'Is the Silverlake gone?'

'The Silverlake Ballroom? My dear man, the Silverlake is gone for twenty years.'

'Tis a garage now,' said Keohane, 'a Toyota dealership. Good bargains there too.'

'That's where we learned about the birds and the bees,' said Bill. He was slightly uncomfortable with the conversation, trying to reach for common ground.

'The Silverlake Ballroom,' said Joey...'d'you remember the night you got stuck in a fight over the Hennessy girl with the fellas from Bantry.'

'I do,' said Bill, 'I was about eighteen, just finished the Leaving Cert. Weren't we celebrating?' He tried to conjure up the face of the teenage hairdresser who raised the blood of all the young men at the dance and set them at each other's throats like stags in spring.

'You were the lucky man I was behind you that night,' said Joey, 'or you'd have been carried out on a stretcher, or maybe a coffin.'

'Quite right,' said Bill in a haze.

'And that wasn't the only time I saved your ass,' said Joey and gave Bill an arch look as his nose twitched. Bill stole an uncomfortable look in his direction.

'The Silverlake was some spot,' said Keohane with gravitas, mopping the counter.

'For Christ's sake,' said Joey, 'didn't you have the best bands in the country playing in the Silverlake: The Dixies, Billy Brown and the Freshmen...'

'Joe Dolan...'

'The Royal,' added Joey, 'Brendan Bowyer and The Royal:

' *"Do the hucklebuck, do the hucklebuck,*
If you don't know how to do it then you're outa luck..." '

He sang in a hoarse, cracked, tuneless voice and then said: 'But you're the man for the singing Bill, give us a blast of *Wooden Heart.*' Bill smiled ruefully and said: 'I haven't sung that song for twenty years.'

'There's no doubt you're some bollocks,' said Joey again, 'what a waste of talent.' And he said to the barman: 'You should have seen this fellow when he was a young blade, Jack Doyle wasn't in it, wouldn't hold a candle to him. And he sang again:

"Can't you see I love you please don't break my heart in two,
That's not hard to do cos I don't have a wooden heart..."'

Bill felt like he was being pulled back into a place where the sun shone bright all around him, when he was nineteen and the son of the morning star. The golden boy of the surrounding territory and all the girls in thrall; asked to sing at every concert and cockfight, and dance at every crossroads and ballroom of romance. The life and soul of every party, liked and praised by older boys and girls. On magic Sundays dancing the night away, basking in the glow of admiring glances. Lines of love-lorn girls with powder and lipstick, drinking bottles of orange juice, locked in lines of rigid segregation, ogling him across the dance floor. Oh, how sweet it was to pretend to be a big shot for an hour or two, stealing furtive, hard-won kisses. Inveigling some forward-thinking girl outside to loiter under a wanton moon, the music of the band floating across the car park, hard chaws smoking in the shadows. Boastful claims of conquest that proved insubstantial in the bright light of day, giving the impression that he had prospects, was going places. But always found out in the end, seen through, intentions queried, amorous advances cut off midstream. It was always thus with poor boys, always would be. The rich girls whom he seemed to favour did not favour him. His pockets weren't deep enough, his education stopped at eighteen. And so he'd wend his weary way homeward and dream of a better life, with big motor cars, swimming pools and girls in bikinis, like Elvis in G.I. Blues.

'Bill Cassidy,' Joey was saying to the barman, 'Bill Cassidy could have been in pictures, should have been. But you know what this fellow's problem was, I'll tell you straight, too easily distracted, too fond of the babes.' And he gave Bill a dig in the ribs and drank again. And both drank again and there followed a silence that might have been too painful to break, that was full of old secrets, angers, maybe betrayals. For the road back home was hard to follow but the road downhill was an easy road that wound with a swift descent. Would that be the road they would go?

'Where are you nowadays, Bill?' asked Keohane politely, 'Dublin, is it?'

'Dublin mostly,' answered Bill and did not elaborate.

'Dublin and everywhere else,' said Joey, and Bill thought he detected a note of pride in his voice, 'this fellow is like J.P. McManus or Magnier, he's always flying in from somewhere.'

'I wish I had their money,' laughed Bill.

'You lived in America for awhile, didn't you,' said Keohane.

'We both did,' said Bill, and he clapped Joey again on the back.

'Really, and what did ye do there?'

'Oh, this and that, we were in Los Angeles, for awhile, San Franscisco too.'

'We were in Berkeley,' said Joey with a wheezing laugh.

'Cripes were ye?'

'We used to walk through the campus every day.'

'By God,' said Keohane.

'That's right,' said Joey, 'on our way to the building site!' Joey thought this hilariously funny and laughed loud and long. Then he said: 'But I came home out of it. Too big for me, this fellow lasted a good bit longer.'

'What's Hollywood like?' asked Keohane.

'A great place if you're doing well,' said Bill, 'not so great if you have to sing for your supper.'

'And did you?'

'What, sing? Oh I did, and got a few small parts in pictures.' Bill said this so casually that the barman, though all agog, thought he must be joking. 'I'm not joking,' laughed Bill, 'I only wish I was more successful at it.'

'Hollywood,' repeated Keohane, unable to compre-hend the concept, 'tis hard to believe someone from around here went to Hollywood, not to mind being in pictures.'

'There you are,' said Bill and smiled a world-weary smile.

'This fellow has what you might call a chequered history,' said Joey cryptically.

'No more than your own,' laughed Bill.

'Yerra God help us, sure when I came back from California I never left again. Oh, I went through the motions at the university, but that was about it. After that I hardly ever left West Cork except to go to the city for the county final.'

'For a man who never went anywhere you know a lot about everything, me included.'

'That's his job, to find out about things,' said Keohane, 'the finest reporter in this part of the country, one of the top men with *The Chronicle*. He has about ten letters after his name you know.' The academic qualification still meant a great deal to the bucolic mind.

'A fat lot of good they are to me,' shrugged Joey, 'an undiscovered Homer, that's what they'd call me around here, if they knew who Homer was,' and he was off laughing at his own graveyard wit again.

'You never lost it' said Bill.

'Never found it you mean,' said Joey with a sad look and shook his resigned head. The drink was making him maudlin. He looked at Bill and looked away again: 'Some of us never made it, never played for Cork.'

'We never made the big money,' added the barman inclining his head toward Bill.

'Never married the beauty queen,' shrugged Joey and stared hard at Bill for some moments. Bill shifted uncomfortably on his feet. 'The beauty queen of Santa Monica,' continued Joey cryptically.

'Never heard of her,' said Keohane, looking from one of them to the other.

'You wouldn't have known her,' said Joey, 'but this man knew her well.' Bill took another drink and put the pint on the counter. He didn't take Joey's bait. 'Christ, we're not finished yet,' he said, 'where's your spirit man?'

'Indeed we are,' said Joey sadly, 'you'd want to have it all done by twenty-five, all behind you by twenty-five.'

There was a long pause as a dripping tap made the only sound in the gloom. The turned down TV screen flickered its jaded images of soccer players and muffled, clichéd commentary.

'Time moves fast,' said Keohane.

'Like a shot,' said Joey, 'and for some of us it might as well have been standing still; but you made the best of it, Bill, you didn't let anything hold you back.' Joey's phrase was pregnant with double meaning.

'You've seen a fair share of the world,' said Keohane, regarding Bill with a mixture of awe and suspicion. Keohane in the manner of the successful but cunning peasant was a man who didn't let his true feelings show at any stage.

'I have,' said Bill.

'And which part did you like the best?'

Bill thought for a moment and then leant on the bar and said: 'You mightn't believe this, but of all the places I've been I like this place best of all.' Joey looked incredulously at him and gave a snort: 'Like hell you do.'

'I never thought I'd think it, or say it for that matter, but it's the truth,' said Bill.

Joey stood up and said he was going to water the pony. As he weaved uncertainly towards the toilets three young men came in and he nearly bumped into them, knocking over a chair. Joey stopped and stared after them. 'Watch where ye're going ye quislings,' he muttered. The young men shrugged and smiled, ignoring him. The barman walked up along the bar towards them and took their order. They were in their late twenties or early thirties, dressed in blue jeans, work boots, T shirts, blouson denim jackets. One was tall, with dark, curling hair, handsome, brown-eyed. One of the others was fair with long flowing locks and the other had his hair in a pony tail. They had a look about them as if they weren't natives of the locality, yet spoke perfect English.

'Americans,' said Keohane as he came back down the bar and Joey returned, smiling a kind of mystical, peaceful smile, as if he were already looking into the next life. 'Things are grand around here,' he said, and then his visage clouded as he looked at the newcomers up the bar.

'Correction,' he said, 'things used to be grand around here, until lately.'

'Shush, Joey, shush,' said the barman under his breath, 'no need to be like that now.'

'What's the matter with you?' said Joey, 'ashamed to call ourselves Irish now are we? Afraid we'll insult the poor immigrants? ...who'd knock you down if you let them, and walk all over you. We had enough of that under the English.' And he raised his voice so that it could be heard around the bar.

'What's wrong with the English?' asked Bill. Joey turned on him and raised a mocking eyebrow. 'It's easy to see you've sold out anyway,' he said. Joey's mood had become volatile all of a sudden.

'Really,' said Bill evenly, 'how's that?'

'Dealing with the English leaves its mark, has always done.'

'What sort of mark?' asked the barman. Joey was

getting more agitated. 'The English,' he burst out, 'the English are a race of shopkeepers, and quislings, they've lost their bottle, their religion, their identity. And we're quickly following them. In fact you could ask, what's the difference anymore between us and them?' He turned back to Bill. 'What's the difference between you and an English capitalist? No difference. You've sold out your father's ideals, and not for the first time either. A landlord, that's what you've become. A fucking landlord. Well, I say the devil take you for your greed that made you sell to Satan.'

'Come on now Joey,' said Bill, 'you're exaggerating a bit.'

'Exaggerating?' said Joey, 'like hell I am. I'm dead serious. The English are a bunch of lousers, and that's my final word on it.' There was a stunned pause and then Keohane said to Bill by way of cooling the sudden increase in temperature. 'Were you ever in France by the way?'

'I was,' said Bill.

'May the Lord forgive you then,' retorted Joey, morosely. Bill laughed: 'And why in the world do you say that?'

'The fucking French are worse than the English,' said Joey. 'Cowardly bastards. At least the Brits went to Iraq. There's nothing in France but poseurs making porno movies and spouting bogus philosophy. Did you ever see their talk shows? A bunch of lechers, ah, meurd…' And he made a face in the French manner, shrugging his shoulders and blowing through his lips. 'As for the Americans,' he continued deliberately raising his voice, 'the Americans are the worst of the lot.' Keohane made a desperate hand motion to Joey to keep his voice down, putting his fingers to his lips.

'Those fellas are Americans,' he whispered, 'will you hold your tongue, man?'

Joey continued, undeterred: 'The Americans have ruined the world. No wonder everyone hates them. Arrogant bastards, spreading every kind of debased filth and debauchery around like slurry on a green field. Selling guns to every side in every conflict around the world. Serves them right their own guns are being used against them now in Iraq and Afghanistan. And I don't care how long you were over there among them either; or how many of our own people are over there. They think they can dictate to us, use us as catspaws.' Then he said, turning back to Bill, 'In fact it would be more in your line to have attended to your obligations over there if you were so fond of them, instead of leaving the dirty washing with me.' And Joey, drank again and his nose began to twitch and his lips curled in a mean line. 'Ah Joey, you've lost the run of yourself completely now,' said Keohane, 'sure you're talking gobbledy-gook now.'

'This fellow knows what I'm talking about,' said Joey mysteriously and said no more. As some other customers came in Bill saluted some of them and the barman greeted some customers he knew. A man came over to shake hands with Bill and said he had seen him mentioned in some television programme or another. They chatted for a few minutes and then the man saluted Joey and moved back to his party. Bill finally turned back to Joey and said: 'What have you been at yourself anyway, Joey, since we spoke last?'

'Devil a much then,' said Joey, 'apart from writing the odd column for *The Chronicle*.'

'That's a good paper,' said Bill. 'I get it sometimes, since it went national. But I thought you were going to get into business there for awhile. Didn't your father want you to take over his law practice?'

'Me, a lawyer?' laughed Joey, 'what d'you call that briefless barrister in *A Tale of Two Cities...Sydney Carton?* That's me. That would be about the long and the short of it as far as my legal career was concerned. No, couldn't imagine myself kissing judges' asses all day long. I tried it for awhile after I came home, but the younger brother took it up. I let him have the business when the father died.' His nose twitched as he sized Bill up again: 'And besides a push from the grave never did anyone any good. No, my heart was never in it, so I stayed here close to home, mornings, evenings, nights. I'd listen to the river flowing and watch the grass grow. I'd hear dogs barking and I'd see bats, night owls.'

'Night owls is right,' laughed Keohane, 'you changed to the right profession for that anyway.'

'You'd be surprised what you'd see at three a.m,' said Joey, 'you'd get plenty of ideas for articles at that hour of the morning. I'd read a bit of Homer maybe when I couldn't sleep. Or I'd wander as far as the foot of Mount Gabriel and I swear I could hear the old heroes crossing the fields with bandoliers and rifles at the trail: the boys who beat the Black and Tans, they were the men, eh? Not a couple of *súmaires* like us.'

'Maybe twasn't the old heroes you saw some of the

time?' said Keohane with a grin and winked at Bill, 'maybe twas a more recent vintage?'

'You know, Jim, if wit was shit you'd be constipated,' said Joey with a sour scowl. Bill waited for some minutes before speaking: 'In the old days we had nothing, but maybe we were as happy as we are today.'

'Well,' said Joey, 'we're all back here where we started from anyway, you with all your *gaisces* and successes, not to mention your money, and me without a shilling. It's like, the faster we go the slower we get or something.' And Joey thought all this very funny and laughed his wheezing, ironic, bittersweet laugh that fell on strangers' and ghosts' ears in the shadows.

> ' *"Oh to be back now, in Carrigfergus,*
> *On that long mountain road down to the sea,"* '

Bill sang the lines with the sweet, clear voice of his youth. Joey said: 'That's beautiful...soft and dolorous; reminds me of sometimes when I see the school children coming through the barley with the afternoon sun on their faces in June and I wish we were young again.' Bill stared fondly at him and was sad for a stymied heart and a man who could paint with words. Joey continued: 'Ah, no, I was never like you, Billy boy, I didn't have the go in me, or maybe I was afraid; whatever it was I'd have to steel myself against the long nights, the boredom with nothing happening. There was very little excitement here after America; everything seemed small, narrow-minded, mundane. But the strain of America was too much. I couldn't stick it.'

'The strain of what?' asked Bill.

'Well, let's say you looked at things differently to me. You could drive on, up the middle, leave people behind you if you had to. No bother to you. But I couldn't leave people behind, especially women. So I came home. My mother was getting on. She needed me, and I suppose I needed her; she ironed my clothes til I was nearly thirty. So I settled for putting a few bob on the horses, building up my record collection: I have every album Bruce Springsteen recorded. Of course I missed the friends we left behind in California. So did you, I expect?' Bill nodded but didn't want to go there. The barman went over to light the electric fire in the open hearth. It glowed like a distant quasar. They were lost in reverie.

Bill had no mother to tell him change his clothes. She died when he was ten and her loss left an indelible mark on him. But that was a loss he buried as he would thenceforth bury all further losses. Maybe he felt rudderless with only the harsh but well-intentioned hand of his father Tom to guide him. Joey lived in a large solicitor's house as big as a presbytery on the edge of the town, but things with Bill and Tom were rough and ready. Away out on a farm, sowing potatoes and ploughing fields with heavy horses, and later a rickety old Ferguson tractor. Hoeing sugar beet in springtime and his fingers freezing as he pulled the heavy beets in bleak, sleet-blown November. Rising early to help Tom with the pigs and calves and then cycling to the bus for secondary school. Back home at five as the routine began again. Often envying Joey the nice, middle class life, the extra money, the home comforts. Then finishing the Leaving Cert. and time hurrying faster and he getting no younger or no richer. The attractions of the Silverlake waning; dented by rejections, disappointments, false promises. Rising twenty and the roles of father and son long since reversed. Now he called the shots and gave the orders: 'Shut up you old fool, what do you know? Stop slobbering your tea in that saucer.' And poor Tom with no choice but to be quiet and do as he was bid. Pushing seventy-five and becoming weak and stumbling, becoming an old man. And Bill all he had. And the young man's restless heart: fighting his chains, his head filled with fantasies of what the world might hold, what the future could bring if only he took wing.

Joey was saying something about a grave. 'What?' asked Bill, jolted back to the present.

'I said it before and I'll say it again, a push from the grave never helped anyone,' said Joey.

'What do you mean a push from the grave?' asked Bill.

'Well, like you got?'

'What did I ever get that I didn't earn?' asked Bill, now suddenly annoyed.

'I'm not saying you didn't earn what you got, but twas the way you went about it,' said Joey sagely.

'I don't know what the hell you're talking about quite frankly,' said Bill, becoming more agitated. His meetings with Joey often ended like this. Too much drink, old coals raked over.

'Sure the whole world knows what I'm talking about.' said Joey.

'Well if it does why don't you spit it out?' said Bill
getting ready to leave. 'There's plenty I could say,' said
Joey, a little smugly, 'but many things are better left
unsaid.'

'Why don't you say one of them at least?'

'No point in opening Pandora's Box now, Billy old
boy. But let's start with the minor item of how you dealt
with your father after he gave you the farm.'

'It's easy for you to sit there and play judge and jury,'
said Bill sarcastically, 'you who had everything handed
to you on a plate all your life. Born with a silver spoon
in your mouth, isn't that what they say.'

Bill felt uneasy. He didn't need this. Joey's eyes
searched for further mischief. Bill drained the last of his
glass and looked at his watch. He slapped Joey on the
shoulder with an old familiar touch and said he'd better
be going. Joey turned to face him fully and bit his tongue
and said no more. Bill then saluted Keohane who had
been trying to hover out of hearing but who had heard
everything: 'Goodnight Bill, good to meet you after all
these years,' he said, 'when will we be seeing you again?'

'I'll be back in the new year,' said Bill, 'three or four
months.'

'Be sure to call then.'

'I will,' said Bill, and looked around and waved at the
customers he knew. As he walked out he caught the eye
of the dark-haired American and nodded.

'Goodnight,' said the American and smiled an open,
cheerful smile.

Bill paused and stretched out his hand, 'Bill Cassidy,'
he said, 'welcome to this part of world.'

'Thanks,' said the young man, 'I'm George Conklin, this is Peter McGregor, and Andy Blair.' Bill shook each of their hands before walking through the door. When he had gone Joey asked for another drink and Keohane said: 'That rattled him a bit. Maybe you were too hard on him?'

'I didn't say anything that hasn't already been said before,' said Joey, 'he'll get over it. He's a hardy boy.'

'That's some car he's driving,' said Keohane, looking out the window as Bill drove off, 'a hundred grand's worth anyway.'

'That's only small change to our Bill,' said Joey.

Twilight was nearly gone and night was falling as Bill left the town and drove on slowly. As the road rose, like a rising crane shot in a movie, a spectacular panorama of sea, islands, castles and boats appeared in breathtaking clarity. How well he knew this view, but each time he returned it became more deeply etched on his psyche. Here is where he felt most real. There were the Skeams, Hare Island, Carthys Islands, Sherkin, and the round camel-hump of Cape Clear on the horizon. And down the long bay, subdivided by serried lines of fish-farming nets, his eyes were carried to the proud, high Fastnet Rock whose lighthouse flashed a welcome to weary sailors all night long. On the foreshore two dark seabirds broke the stillness with lonesome cries. And flew.

There were several new houses on the old road since last he ventured down this way. Some were big, stone-faced mansions, the likes of which only wealthy Germans could once afford but which probably now belonged to some Irishman from Dublin, made good like himself. There were new, plainer bungalows too, built by the locals. You could tell. The outsiders could afford a bigger splash, a finer finish. The locals found it hard to compete despite the boom times. The rich were getting richer, where once a thousand died from famine in every household as far as the eye could see. But those tragedies were best forgotten, erased from memory. The march was onward, upward, a rising tide to lift all boats.

When he came to his own place he got quite a shock. The farmyard was gone, the old famine cottage gone, and the house where he was born transformed from a standard, plastered, three-bedroomed country farmhouse into something strange and out of place and new, with towers, and balconies and arches. A hodge-podge of fake Georgian pillars, Corinthian columns and balustrades that might have suited Malibu or Miami-Dade County but looked like a malevolent Hogwarts here from the tales of Harry Potter. The surrounding field where the heavy horses used to graze was now a wide, green lawn and the front garden was a riot of alien shrubbery with names he could only guess at. Oh, this was home no more. Hard as he looked he could uncover no trace of his childhood, all vanished like a slate wiped clean. A large Mercedes was parked inside the huge electronic gates on the tarred yard. Two fearsome bald eagles stood sentry on two enormous pillars which proclaimed that the person who now lived here was richer, better, more beautiful, could travel further, fly faster, was lord of all he surveyed.

He debated with himself whether to go in to introduce himself, but if the inside was like the outside then all vestiges, all traces, all shadows of Bill Cassidy, his father Tom, and his mother Mary and the hard-scrabble life they led would surely have been consigned to oblivion, with not even a photograph to record that they had ever been here at all. Such a trauma he chose not to face. He still had his memories, his regrets, his subterranean pain. While he had them he was still alive, though running on empty for a good while now.

He drove on slowly up the hill past the house and attempted to shrug off those tears of regret, tears of time. When he came to the last field where the bounds ditch ran he got out and looked back down at the buildings nestling in the valley under the hill. He could hear like only yesterday his father's voice as he came across the farmyard that rainy, long gone day as Bill was finishing the milking, and his father saying: 'I've made the place over to you,' And Bill stopping, surprised, and saying: 'What?'

And Tom saying: 'I went to Crowley, the solicitor, I signed it over to you, lock, stock and barrel.'

'You did?'

'I did, for better or for worse, tis done now.'

And Bill remembered staring into the future as a pride of hungry cats nearly upscuttled a bucket of milk and he kicking them away. A whirlwind of thoughts going through his head. His place now? Was this a bribe, or worse, maybe a trap? What about his hatching plans for leaving, and the bright lights and the big city? But only saying: 'That's fine so,' and then straining the warm, creamy milk into the shining, silver churn, watching the froth collecting in bubbles as the milk gurgled, sang as it hit the bottom. Smelling the sweet, green-grass tang of the milk and licking a glob of fresh cream from his fingers.

As he stood looking down at the new order, the new monstrosity where his old life used to be, Joey Harrison's final rebuke went round his head and random memories continued to hit him thick and fast.

After Tom's unexpected gesture a noticeable springing in his step. His voice echoing in song across the townlands like the voice of Orpheus singing to light up the gloom of the approaching winter. And winter coming in like a lion, coming in to kill. Howling gales in November, trees falling and the roads becoming rivers, swept away. December and hard frosts and the peeping call of the plover, and the whirring wings of the jacksnipe sending out a goat's song: *an gabhairín rua.* Frozen lakes, dead birds on ice for want of water:

> "A bhonnáin bhuí se mo léan the luí,
> Is do chnámha sínte tar éis do ghrinn."

In the snows of January cattle hungry in the uplands, Bill struggling through snowdrifts to feed the bellowing beasts. His fingers frostbitten, icicles on his nose, his elation on becoming a landowner quickly dissipating in the cold winds of reality blowing against his backside month after month. Surely there was a better life? He had heard there was money to be made in Boston and New York. Maybe even out in California. There was a company in Cork near the University sending students out on summer jobs and they came back loaded. And he could afford to go now. Better still, he had an asset to realize. And if things didn't work out he could live on the money, or maybe parlay it into millions. The path to freedom suddenly seemed rosy.

The unthinkable was already foremost in his mind before he was consciously aware of it, and then quietly rationalizing the betrayal of his father. The deal done with a man from the next parish before telling Tom. Choosing a man who was fond of money and land, who valued land over loyalty. Some others might have baulked at the suggestion, indeed some were scandalized, like Joey Harrison's father. Some old comrades of Tom Cassidy who remembered the struggles he came through refusing to speaking to Bill again. And Bill gone with the money almost before anyone was aware that he had sold the farm. Eaten bread was soon forgotten, and first on the narrow streets of Cork, and giddy with Eileen McManus in the clubs of San Francisco and Los Angeles the pain and loneliness of a grand old man walking by the sea was not something to be dwelt on over-long. Summer was coming, then winter, then another summer and Bill would be coming home. But not yet, not yet. Where had all the years gone and whither all the money? A cache of money leaving his pockets like leaves from a beech tree in the first autumn storm. The singing, and the dancing and romancing. London, and Paris and out to California. Time hurrying, years passing. Even Eileen soon forgotten.

The wind was rising, rain was on that wind. He got back in the car and drove down to the foreshore. The past and the present now all coalescing in his mind. Old Tom

dying and he standing at the grave talking to the dead.
And furtive recriminating eyes. Leaving his father to be
cared for by strangers and his father lonesome for his
son's return. The old hero: the man who fought for his
country. Tears of guilt every time he stood in
conversation with the dead, everyone he knew as a boy
now dead, the dead more real than the living. And the
one beautiful ghost who would not die.

Out along the bay the high cliffs of Cape Clear hulked
somewhere in the darkness gathered around him. An
enormous darkness swept every now and then by the
slender, white pencil of the Fastnet Light. He walked,
cloaked from disapproving eyes and the torment of Joey's
undeniable accusation. And then his fingers felt the
solid, reassuring pier. He heard small boats bobbing and
clunking against each other on the rising tide. And the
smell of fuchsia and deadly nightshade brought him
peace by these untrammelled waters until he could no
longer hear the sorrowing cries of those dark birds of
shame.

CHAPTER 4

curmudgeonly coats

Joey Harrison rolled over on his sagging mattress and wondered whether to get up? Rainy weather, windy and damp. You got that around the equinox. The alarm had gone off and he'd ignored it. As usual. What was there to get up for? Resolutions came and went but the fire in his belly around midnight was a cold, dead thing at eight a.m. Bill Cassidy always brought out the best and the worst in him. He felt a bit guilty now. Maybe he'd been a bit too hard on him. Ah, the hell with him. He could take care of himself. He'd been in long pants a good while now. Probably gone back to Dublin already without a second thought. Should he give him a call? Where was his mobile phone number? He sat up and flicked through his diary for it. Not there for some reason. Ah, fuck it, it could wait. Still it was nice to see his old friend every now and again. But was friend really

the word anymore? As we grow older we're less forgiving
of our old friends. We pull our curmudgeonly coats more
tightly around us. Yes, he thought, that was a good word,
curmudgeonly.

The old four poster was warm but he knew cold
breezes blew in through every crevice in the high-
ceilinged bedroom. Downstairs the fire would be gone
out. He had no wife, no cleaner, no dog. The damp
insinuated in through every wall, ran down in rivers over
window panes. He turned over and reached for his half-
completed article for *The Chronicle*. They were used to
his deadline coming and going. But they waited for him
because Joey Harrison was full of ire and spite and
vinegar. The readers liked that in these parts.

He threw his legs out and padded barefoot in his shirt
and underwear to take a leak in the toilet. How old were
these Belfast sinks and bowls and baths? There in his
father's time, grandfather's: relics of old decency. He
leant against the high window sill in the manner of a
drunk, supporting himself with his elbow and the back of
his hand up against his forehead. He was cold, stone
sober but his head ached from last night's excesses. As
his water hissed in a rushing, filamented arc into the
bowl he could see through the fogged-up window
headstones leaning over, urns, great tombs, sarcophagi,
mausoleums: defaced with seagulls droppings. The
Harrison family were all buried in that old graveyard on
the banks of the Ilen river. Beside Wolfes, Cavendishes,
Chineries. What the hell half of them were you never
could tell: Protestant, Catholic, dissenter? Some took
the soup, some went the other way and became apostates

like his own crowd. Some were bastards, some turncoats, others heroic old Republicans. A long line all the way down from 1798 to 1916, through the Fenians and young Irelanders and the Famine. All now equal in the dust. The view was good up towards Oldcourt and Skibbereen where the river widened out in a great looping bend. If you panned your eyes from left to right you beheld the river in full spate gliding down the sweeping estuary to Reengaroige, Turk Head, and turning out to sea past the Lousy Rocks, Baltimore and Sherkin. What good were views for those who were sleeping? The sleep from which there was no waking? He still could see that view from the great windows of the old house. But father, mother no longer could.

Down in the huge, old kitchen he boiled up the kettle and reheated yesterday's porridge in the microwave. The comforts of modern conveniences. He rarely lit the iron Wellstood range, except to heat the hot water for a bath, and that a rare experience. He got the whiff of body odour as he turned off the last step of the stairs and nearly shocked himself. Always a surprise to sniff your own sour redolence. The wind and rain of last night had finally opened a large chink in one of the beautiful, arched Georgian windows and there was a pool of water on the floor. He searched out yesterday's *Times* and used it as a mat. As good a use for it as any. He was getting more and more annoyed at its leader writer's tone of bleeding liberalism. How long before these people realized what was going on in this little country?

He turned on his laptop and checked to see the printer was connected. He reprinted the pages:

"Eighty thousand immigrants a year, documented and otherwise flood into Ireland. That's eight hundred thousand in ten years. Is anyone doing the math? How long before this island's tiny population is no longer fully Irish…?"

He reread the piece and tried to collate his thoughts. This was always the hardest part. Facing the half-printed page. This was the spade work: hard as hewing wood and drawing water. What was he trying to establish? How would he put it? That it was argued by academics how outsiders were always absorbed into the Irish race, the DNA was too strong to be diluted? Yes of course, but that was before instant communication, daily flights and ferries; when people came up the rivers like the Ilen and the Bandon in dugouts and canoes, and hunted wolves and wild boar in the forests. A slow process unwinding over centuries. Nowadays in every town in West Cork you heard accents from Poland, Russia, Lithuania, Latvia, Spain. Whatever became of the ancient Erse? Yes, that might look good put down in words. He began tapping and thought: a plague on them all. And slurped his coffee. At least his editor was a man after his own heart. This piece should pass muster without much trouble. He was glad he didn't have to write for *The Times*. Political correctness he could do without.

Half an hour later he was walking up the main street with his old overcoat buttoned to his chin and his copy folded in his inside pocket. The Iarnród Éireann bus was blocking a long line of cars as usual and there was that self-important film actor making outraged gestures at the driver who shrugged and laughed back at him. Served him right. Who did these fellows think they were? Because they made a few movies people like Joey and the bus driver were supposed to genuflect before them. A particularly attractive young solicitor in a pinstripe suit with her hair tied in a bun passed him and gave a dazzling smile. Wouldn't mind giving her one at lunchtime.

The midday crowd at the new restaurant always contained a fugitive or two. Across the river and into the car park behind the supermarket. As usual a damned hippie with an estuary accent refusing to yield her parking space to the line of cars behind her. Her pony-tailed boyfriend who worked on that pink castle out in the bay giving the finger to the honking motorists. Arrogant Brits, what did they think this was, 1900? At least the *Celtic Tiger* had put that lot in their place. Any number of local Irish businessmen would now buy and sell them all before breakfast. That thought always gave him a frisson of satisfaction. Tables turned. Like that house painter fellow whom he was convinced was ex SAS. Probably murdered somebody. Got his walking papers no doubt. Hiding out in the boondocks with the Paddys. Thinks he's not noticed? Did they all think West Cork was on the moon? Joey Harrison notices everything.

The food in Shorten's supermarket was scrumptious. Devilled eggs, stuffed vine leaves and sundried tomatoes. He was becoming addicted to those. He sauntered over to the wine section and surveyed the selection. This Shorten fellow hadn't bad taste. He was bent over reading a label when a forty-something with dyed blonde hair pushing a heaving trolley nearly ran him over. Not so much as an excuse-me as she muscled in beside him. Oh, they all loved their Merlots and Cab Savs, that crowd some writer had nicknamed, *The Pope's Children*. You saw them on Saturdays, down for the weekend from Cork and Dublin, in deck shoes, no socks and shorts. Sailing in Baltimore and Schull. Could they tell a Chateaux Margaux from a Pomerol? A Crozes-Hermitage from a Beaujolais Villages? In a pig's eye.

Maybe he'd pick a nice Cote du Rhone himself? He liked the Southern Rhone: Chateauneuf Du Pape. He might stretch to that. Light up the old stove and invite someone out. Who could he think of? That widow with the three rebellious teenagers was gone off him. No chance with the nubile solicitor. Knew her father too well. Maybe the one who sang Danny Boy and applied the Johnsons baby oil: that *Molly Bloom* of Carberey's Hundred Isles? Hadn't seen her for awhile. She was usually hot to trot. Did he have her phone number? Hmm.

'Joey, how are you this afternoon?' Someone clapped him on the shoulder. Murphy, the real estate man with the searching eyes who always looked you up and down in a slightly deploring fashion, making you conscious of your frayed collar and shabby shoes. And he immaculate in a light-grey pinstripe. Very tall and thin with an aristocratic stoop, brown, laced-up Barkers, the best of British leather.

'Hey, Michael, thank God it's Friday.'

'Not that it matters to you,' said Murphy, ever so

slightly deprecating, 'every day is Friday to Joey Harrison.'

'A fair point, Michael, a fair point.'

'Are you going to the Council meeting over at the Devonia?'

'I might, must drop my copy off first at *The Chronicle*.'

'You should email that,' said Murphy.

'Wouldn't know how,' said Joey, insouciantly.

'The meeting should be rousing,' said Murphy.

'What's on the agenda?' Joey asked.

'We're trying to get that new development down on Turk Head voted through. I'd say we'll encounter some tough opposition.'

'Oh, fierce, don't you know. You'll have your work cut out for you with all the blow-ins around here telling us what's good for us.'

'Can we count on your support?' asked Murphy.

'Naturellement,' said Joey, 'I always like a good scrap with that Green crowd.' Murphy loped off. Joey stood looking after him. Very plausible, Michael Murphy, when he needed something from you. Where'd he get that urbane accent? And the way he narrowed his eyes; and that sensitive, mobile mouth. Wonder was he a closet queen? A secret shafter? But how much backbone would he have when the chips were really down? Could Joey count on him then? Never a great man under the high ball? Suspect in that department. Still, he's one of us.

'Who's doing the math as the Yanks always say? That's good, I like that, Joey.' said Tim Durkin.

'Thought you might,' said Joey.

'But a bit of an exaggeration. No?'

Tim Durkin, the editor of *The Chronicle* was in blue shirtsleeves, belt and braces, sitting behind his massive walnut desk, where he sat all day munching biscuits. Dust and paper everywhere. Durkin had soft skin, a long, pointed nose and a double chin. Everything about him said soft. Gave the impression of being fatter than he actually was. Must suffer from flatulence after all those biscuits. Had he blood pressure?

'I wouldn't say it's a million miles from the truth, Tim,' said Joey, 'and even if it's not eighty thousand per annum it soon will be at the rate things are going. What have we here, four million? In twenty years half of us will be speaking some form of Polack.'

'Better than speaking Urdu,' said Durkin.

'Well, whatever. Where do they speak that, Morrocco?'

'Morrocco, Libya, somewhere over there.'

'Have I made my point?'

Durkin stood and brushed a shower of dry scalp skin off his shoulders. Psoriasis? Must be under pressure?

'Alright, Joey,' he said, 'we'll run with it and see what happens. And let me know how the UDC meeting goes this afternoon. If there are fireworks we want it on the front page. Something immediate, juicy.'

Joey and Durkin had negotiated their way from Durkin's glass-partitioned inner office to the main door past several pale-skinned typists hunched over desks. Durkin put his hand on Joey's shoulder. 'By the way, you know this fellow, Bill Cassidy?'

Joey stopped and turned to look straight at him. 'Why wouldn't I know Bill Cassidy?'

'A bit of a high flyer these days by all accounts,' said Durkin.

'As high as they come,' replied Joey.

'Where'd he get all his money?'

'How d'you mean?' asked Joey.

Durkin leant in to Joey's left ear and lowered his voice. 'This is confidential, but I hear, through the grapevine, that he's up before one of those Tribunals in Dublin in the not too distant future.'

'So, they'll find nothing. Bill is clever. Cunning as a shit-house rat.'

'He's got this fancy hotel outside of Cork, down Kinsale way,' continued Durkin, 'a five star, though I've never been there. That, by all accounts might be a source of interest. Would you ever do a bit of, ah... research, let's call it?'

Joey paused, and looked momentarily agitated.

'We'd foot the exes for a couple of nights in the lap of luxury,' continued Durkin quickly. Joey cleared his throat and said. 'You know Bill is an old friend of mine, Tim.'

'All the more reason to send you on this mission.' Durkin gave a thin smile as Joey walked through the door.

Half an hour later anyone walking through the lobby of the Devonia Hotel would have heard loud, shouting voices and what sounded like tables being thumped repeatedly coming from somewhere behind a double mahogany door giving into a large conference room.

Inside, a chaotic meeting of the Urban District Council was going at full throttle. There was a committee comprising five people sitting at a long table at the top of the room, which was pretty much packed to capacity down to the door. The Chairman, whose name was Antony Gibson-Fitch, was vainly trying to keep order: a very thin, red-faced man with a hooked nose, aged about sixty-five. He wore a tweed suit, check shirt and cravat, and his surprisingly jet-black hair was parted in the middle and slicked back like an aging screen idol. A debonair hankie flowed out of the top breast pocket of his jacket. But his most significant characteristic was his deeply plummy, Home Counties accent, which he used as a weapon of attack when it suited him, and as an impenetrably high, defensive shield when he wanted to deflect away undue scrutiny. To one such as Joey Harrison, who happened to be duelling with him at the present moment, the accent was a source of complete irritation, notwithstanding the merits of the argument being advanced.

Flanking Gibson-Fitch to his left was the urbane Michael Murphy and to his right sat the fetching young solicitor, Ita Mulcahy. Next to Ita sat a putative film director called Jonathan Keel, another West Brit who spent some time in the southwest and the rest in the Dublin area. He was wearing a rumpled Armani jacket and black T-shirt which stamped him out as being a member of the artistic community whose brainpower and ability was considerably less than the image he would like to portray to the world. The last person in the row was the cagey Jim Keohane who acted as the recording secretary for affairs and who despite his quiet, low-key appearance was the man who kept the whole shambling business together.

Confronting this eclectic assortment of humanity was a very riled up Joey Harrison who was attempting to impose his opinions on the proceedings with a mixture of bluster and guile: 'It's easy for you people to sit up there and pronounce on the aesthetic values of this development. The fact is you don't live here all year round. People have to make a living, life is hard here for six months of the year with no tourists and bills to be paid. Any of you people try living on one of these islands when the cold winds of January are blowing up your backsides.'

'But Mr. Harrison,' said Gibson-Fitch, 'what's proposed here is a substantial mixed development of residential apartments, retail and warehousing that will stick out like a sore thumb in one of the most beautiful coastal stretches, out of all proportion to the surrounding vernacular.'

'Vernacular?' sneered Joey, 'since when has everybody started using the word vernacular? This is some word that a twenty-five year old planner found in the dictionary and decides that it sounds elegant. Why not use the word homely, or bucolic, which is what you really mean?'

'Mr. Harrison, Mr. Harrison,' intervened Keel, the pseudo film director, 'that is not what the Chairman meant at all. You really are putting words in his mouth.'

'And what would you know about it sitting up there with your phoney accent? What the hell have you ever done that entitles you to be on this committee in the first place?'

'I live here... part of the year...' began Keel.

'You live in Killiney you mean and you come down here in July for a few weeks and go to some exclusive barbecues. You're nothing but a kiss-ass. You like to be seen in the company of some very wealthy foreigners who disport themselves here when it suits them and pretend you're one of them and superior to the locals: the vernacular as you'd like to say. Anyway, what films have you ever made? None that I've ever seen.' Joey's tirade was greeted with titters of laughter around the room.

'Mr. Harrison,' said Gibson-Fitch, 'I really must ask you to stick to the subject matter at hand. Mr. Keel's business is not at issue here.'

'Well,' continued Joey, 'I say this development has to be approved for the good of this entire community and for the sake of ensuring continued employment in the area and the prevention of job losses and the disruption of families.'

'What the Chairman was suggesting, if I understand him, is that perhaps some modification in the plans might go some way to having this matter pass the motion here today,' said Michael Murphy, full of smiles and sniffs of camaraderie to Gibson-Fitch.

'You don't quite have me there, Mr. Murphy,' said the Chairman quickly, 'no, I cannot say as I can agree in any way with this development taking place at the particular location in question, or any coastal location for that matter.'

'But the entire point of the development is that it would be in an area of tourism,' said Keohane. 'With respect Mr. Chairman, a whole new island-to-mainland access point is badly needed and this is the ideal location for it.'

'Well then, why not extend the pier, why do you need a huge apartment development?' said Keel.

'Look,' said Joey, 'it's all very well for you people as I said before. You arrive here like fair weather birds of passage, spend a few euro in the supermarkets and the fancy restaurants and then you leave your holiday monstrosities empty for the rest of the year. You're not really part of this community in any meaningful sense. You cannot dictate to us what we can or cannot do.'

'In fairness, Joey this is a democratic forum,' said Michael Murphy, 'this will be decided on a vote in the long run, including your own.'

'And in fairness to you, Michael you're nothing but a poltroon,' retorted Joey with a gleeful grin. 'Which side are you on anyway? Do you want this project passed or are you just trying to impress Gibson here?'

'Ahem, ah, it's Gibson-Fitch,' said the Chairman.

'I don't care if it's Mel Gibson,' said Joey, 'your stupid double-barrelled name might impress an illiterate like Michael here but it doesn't impress me. You're not as blue-blooded as you would like us to believe. More likely some kind of conman on the run from something over there.'

There was a murmur of dissent from the crowd. Jonathan Keel got very exercised. 'Withdraw that remark,' he expostulated.

'I won't withdraw it,' said Joey, his voice rising, 'if he likes it so much in the Home Counties why doesn't he stay there? More likely they wouldn't have him.'

'I'm afraid you're out of order, Joey,' said Michael.

'Put that man out,' shouted Keel.

'Who's going to put me out?' roared Joey, 'my family have been prominent in this community for four hundred years. We're the Harrisons. We fought in '98 and in 1920. Who'll put a Harrison outside the door? Come on ye quislings.'

There was a melée as a bunch of the Green confraternity came over to assist a policeman in trying to remove Joey. Then came a strong, calm voice, louder than the rest, which caused Joey's lynching party to stop in its tracks. 'Can we hold our horses here a minute?' A tall, dark-haired young man dressed in casual jeans and work boots came forward and stood between Joey and the top table. 'While I'm not familiar with the details of the proposal here I believe a compromise can be arrived at to satisfy all sides.'

A compromise thought Joey, as he stared at this newcomer? Where had he seen this guy before? Yes, last night, in Keohane's pub. Didn't like the look of him there. Still don't.

'What did you have in mind, Mr. ah…?' asked the Chairman.

'Conklin, George Conklin, I'm afraid I'm not from around here, but I've been here long enough to understand what would work and what wouldn't.'

'And where the hell are you from?' asked Joey, hostility dripping from his voice.

'I'm from Los Angeles, California.'

'Another one,' sneered Joey, 'Lord God protect us from the do-gooders of this world. Anyway, what connection do you have to this place that gives you the right to tell us what's good for us?'

'Mr. Harrison, can you let the man speak?' cut in the Chairman loudly.

'You might call me a do-gooder but I'd like to call myself more of a pragmatist, Mr. ah...?'

'Harrison, to you,' said Joey. 'Listen, you're full of crap like the rest of them.'

'You might like to think so, sir, but in the first place I have a direct connection to Ireland because my father came from this locality, and secondly, I've seen enough destructive development in Southern California to persuade me that if it's allowed to go unbridled here you'll destroy the very thing that makes you unique.'

'And what the fuck do you have in mind?' shouted Joey.

'Well, for instance I have just gotten planning permission to build a thatched house up in the mountains and the idea is to do a planned community of such houses which will restore some of the character which has been lost around here.'

'A fucking thatcher?' shouted Joey, 'I bet you had no trouble getting your little cottage passed by the Council.'

'Look,' said George calmly, 'you're not prepared to listen because your personal agenda here today obviously is to use this forum as a battering ram to silence any kind of reasonable objection. Because you really don't want any kind of foreigners here at all.'

'Damn right I don't,' said Joey.

'You're pretty much a bigot aren't you. A racist even.'

'What if I am?' asked Joey, 'because I want to keep Ireland for the Irish? If that makes me a racist fine, I'm a racist. But our fathers fought long and hard to kick the British out of here and we don't want any others taking their place.'

'What I'm talking about is enhancing the landscape. It has nothing to do with past history,' said George.

'Which of those little planners with the tight skirts did you shag to get that one through?' shouted Joey. 'We're being told what's good for us night and day by people so young they believed in Santa Claus only a few years ago...this place is gone to the dogs!'

'That's it,' said the Chairman, 'put that man out!'

With much pushing and shoving and cursing and swearing Joey was manoeuvred slowly towards the door as if caught in the rolling maul of a rugby scrum. He waved his fist at Gibson-Fitch, hurled further insults at Michael Murphy, Keel the failed filmmaker and George Conklin: 'I've never heard of a Conklin in this neck of the woods, a whore's son most likely...go back to your ghetto where you belong.'

George could only shrug and hold out his upturned palms as Joey was eventually ejected on his hands and knees into the lobby and the door slammed in his face. He gave a few running kicks against the outside before feeling his bruised toes and then sloped off out and down the street. His shirt collar was pulled out and torn over and buttons were missing from his long overcoat. He was mouthing furiously to himself. Bemused passersby stared after him in astonishment.

'They've gone too far this time, Jim, I'm telling you someone's going to pay for this.' It was several hours later and Joey was inside in a snug in Jim Keohane's bar after lowering a half bottle of whiskey. His eyes looked bloodshot and he was slurring his words. He slumped over on a small table as Keohane spoke to him through a small opening in the side counter. He looked utterly unkempt and his eyes carried a sense of deep sadness and indefinable loss. He began to shiver. 'I'm telling you, Jim there'll be hell to pay for this.'

'There will, there will,' said Keohane desperate to keep Joey from creating any further mayhem. The main lounge of his bar was full on this Friday night and he had a belligerent Joey penned in the snug without appearing to have him prisoner. He had to keep plying him with liquor.

'But you stood up for me against the dirty bastards,' said Joey darkly, 'you took my side, didn't you Jim?'

'Why wouldn't I?' said Keohane, well aware that at any moment he could find himself on the receiving end of one of Joey's savage rebukes. He had known him for far too long and had felt the lash of his tongue too often to feel complacent in that regard.

'The only decent fucking man among them, boy,' repeated Joey, 'you know Jim Keohane, you're the only man with any backbone in this one-horse town. As for that *sleeveen* Murphy and that fucking Yank. I'm telling you, Jim, that Yank is in for a bit of a surprise one of these nights.' Joey swayed in his seat and winked knowingly at Keohane: 'A big fucking surprise.'

'Listen, Joey,' said Keohane after a long, pregnant pause, 'the squad car is outside. The boys will drop you home. You're in no condition to walk I'd say.'

'The squad is it?' asked Joey, his eyes brightening, 'send them in, I'll stand them a drink. The only bloody men worth buying a drink for in this kip.'

Two tall, powerful policemen came in the side door of the snug from the street. Joey's demeanour changed immediately and he became docile and conciliatory like a lamb. 'Come on,' said Sergeant Sheridan, a tall grey-haired man with deep-set eyes and a large, black moustache.

'Ah, my 'venereal' friends the *gauleiters*,' said Joey sardonically and sat up in his chair: 'The only men between us and the barbarians at the gate. Here have a drink, Sergeant.' Joey lifted the bottle but the Sergeant brusquely took it away from him: 'It's time you went along. You've caused enough mayhem for one day by all accounts.'

'Tim Durkin wanted a juicy story for his front page,' said Joey, 'by Christ he's got it now right enough.' And he burst into one of his self-deprecating, cackling laughs which were always so infectious.

As they drove him home in the squad car down the dark road to the crumbling old *Wuthering Heights* by the graveyard Joey broke into a cracked attempt at a high tenor aria:

"*Dalle stanza, dove Lucia...*"

'Do you know that one Sergeant, the sextet from *Lucia Di Lammermoor,* by Donizetti?' The Sergeant scowled and ignored the question. Joey was becoming more than a thorn in his side and sooner or later Sheridan would have to teach him a lesson. 'Maria Callas, her finest hour,' continued Joey. 'Do you know it young man?'

'I never had the educated tastes of a man like you,' said the young Gárda sarcastically.

'You're too modest young fellow,' said Joey from the back of the car, 'too modest by far. Now come here to me, could anyone of you gentleman make a phone call for me?...on one of those mobile phone things you carry? Here's the number.' Joey leant forward and handed the Sergeant a piece of paper with a woman's name written on it.

'Molly, who?' asked the Sergeant squinting to read it. 'Molly Bloom,' said Joey succinctly, managing to be condescending and benign at the same time, 'Molly Bloom of Carberey's Hundred Isles. Give her a call for me will you?'

'I never heard of her. Is she living around here?'

'Indeed she is, Frank, indeed she is. She's a local model. A bucolic version of the original who was a Dubliner residing in the imagination of James Joyce, and of course you know who he was?' The younger policeman looked at the Sergeant in weary bafflement. The Sergeant's look was one of brooding irritation. He opened the car window and slowly crumpled up the note and threw it out.

CHAPTER 5

a thing of beauty

George Conklin, the young American, stood watching
the river flow. It ran wide and quiet before the bridge.
Deep-coloured, almost black. Black as coal in the
deepest part. It shallowed out towards either bank where
long, green strands of algae, like hair brushed by the
water *(like the tangles of Neaera's hair)* flowed with the
current. On the banks themselves the sedge leant in as if
to caress the ripples, and tall-stalked reeds grew in great
profusion where herons stood still, camouflaged.
Petrified as ancient bog wood. Startled thrushes and
greenfinch flew up and away from a swooping kestrel
with striped undersides and sickle beak: the stealthy
raptor of the skies bearing down upon them into oak and
ash woods further back. Two swans floated upstream
passed by a wary flotilla of ducks, and the young man
looking from the bridge could see the white clouds of the

sky, the silver birches and willows of the nearer bank reflected in the smooth, wide waters. The bridge had three arches with sharp cutwaters on the upper side to keep it from being swept away in a flood. A narrow, tarred road snaked into and over·the bridge and out the other side in the shape of an S. Away southward, high, evergreen-covered hills stood guard over the remnants of the ancient broadleaf woodlands, scattered on the lower slopes below.

It was deathly quiet. George stood and listened and gradually other sounds impinged upon his ears: the churring calls of the swans, higher tweets and chirps of smaller birds, a dog barking somewhere on the barer hills north of the river. He turned to the far parapet, towards the river flowing downstream and gradually the sounds of more turbulent water floated back. This was where the wide stream disappeared in the distance and where the land on either bank went from flat, green fields to rougher brakes and rocky breaknecks descending down in graduated steps. Here the river changed into a white-foamed, capricious flood, dancing and cascading merrily this way and that as long, black, jagged rocks altered its course.

The river was the Bandon and he was near its source. It would eventually flow onward through a rich, wide valley past the raddled towns of Dunmanway, Enniskean, Bandon, Inishannon to the old Spanish-stepped streets of Kinsale many miles away. And finally home to the sea. Far back up the rising tableland the corrugated slopes of a mysterious-looking mountain reached for magnificence. Cone-shaped from a distance,

a pyramid, compelling in its power. This was where the
river rose, flowing out of a black lake at the mountain's
base. The English had called the mountain Owen. He
suspected it meant the more poetic *Abhainn*, the Gaelic
name for river. From the west of this mountain range the
rivers flowed in the opposite direction. The Ilen flowed
south between Bantry and Drimoleague and on through
Skibbereen to reach the sea at Roaringwater Bay. The
Lee further north rose at Gougane Barra and flowed
eastward to Cork City.

He wasn't fluent in Irish but he had come back to find
the place where he belonged. And Ireland was his own
source although California was his birthplace. And these
Caha mountains were now his High Sierras, his Rockies,
his very own Grand Tetons rising to the sky. Not as tall
or vaulting, but each landscape reaches its own plateau,
each mountain range folds into a completeness in itself
with its own grandeur no matter what its height. And
Owen was the monarch here of all that it surveyed. He
smelt the acrid resin of pine, the tangy sweet and sour of
rushy bogland. He plucked a thin, long blade of ripe,
hay-coloured grass and chewed it in his mouth.

He was still in his blue jeans and a blouson jacket and
building boots. He carried himself with an easy, athletic
grace and his hands were calloused from the work he had
been doing. From the harsh crunch of concrete and the
smoother caress of planed beechwood, the mulchier
touch of coppered mountain earth, and fertile,
chocolate-coloured plough-lands between rivers and
mountains.

He turned and walked back over the bridge. He came

to a crossroads and took the southern fork. He passed a wooden school house hidden in the trees adorned with a huge yellow sunflower on its wall. He saluted the few parents waiting for the children to be released. Mostly young, the men were long-haired, some smooth-skinned, some bearded, some with ponytails. Andy Blair and Peter McGregor among their number: all prominent participants in the recent planning debate in the Devonia Hotel in the town. Their clothes were made from natural fibres: wool and cotton, their shoes of Spanish leather. The women were of similar age, bearing and appearance, dressed in coloured skirts and jumpers, with adornments of braids and bangles, some with earrings in their noses, even tongues. Their cars were battered Ford Cortinas, multicoloured Hiace and Volkswagen vans: nothing less than ten years old. But their faces were unusually fresh, unlined by hardship or penury. They looked like extras in a movie playing peasants but unable to hide their bourgeois origins: the flotsam and jetsam of the world's richer countries making common cause in this last pristine wilderness. Intent on rejecting everything their parents built and hoarded: their values of thrift and husbandry; saving the planet and promoting alternative ecosystems. Globalization, economic expansion, the entrepreneurial huffing and puffing that they saw encroaching all around them had no place or welcome here.

George exchanged some pleasantries and walked on and took a dog-leg lane deeper into the hills. Halfway up the deciduous trees thinned out to leave only the gloomy pine and fir and spruce, through which the soft wind soughed. And the ubiquitous thorny furze, with its glorious yellow flowers, now faded, but that would burst out like a supernova across the hillsides in the sweet month of May. Then the trees thinned out and were nearly gone and there was the farmyard in front of him. He was breathless from the climb.

A house half-completed and designed for thatching filled the framed gateway of the yard like a picture from a postcard. It rose from the ruins of another old cottage that had leant over crazily, stone upon stone ready to stagger and fall and that he could not salvage. He had set to work building from the ruins of history and old sorrows, to create a monument to little dead children, old men and women all swept away in the Great Hunger that had ravaged this territory a century and a half ago. He would create a thing of beauty, built the way the old folks built, from native timber, reed and plaster. From clay and stone. And he was already halfway there. A swarthy local man with gentle eyes and great, graceful hands greeted him with a humorous smile: 'Well, Georgie,' how are you today?' This was Cornelius, an artist with trowel, hammer and chisel.

'Good, Cornelius,' George replied, 'I've been to town for some groceries and I brought your favourite streaky bacon for lunch.'

'That's the talk,' said Cornelius, 'all we need now is a bloody whiskey and we're right for road.' George liked Cornelius's company, his sardonic, gentle humour and his ability to work long and steady through the day. When he first broached the idea of building a new thatched structure he was met by a certain amount of scepticism. The idea was outmoded. Modern dwellings were all slate, or tile, but George wanted something to compliment this rugged, rain-kissed landscape, where there was silence and peace, and where the mad, hurrying chariot of twenty-first century development was still a good ways off. He wanted to preserve or recreate the best of what was here before the ghastly bungalows crept up from the lowlands and gobbled the remaining few beautiful fields.

'Thatch is it?' Cornelius had asked with that familiar twinkle in his eye that was unspoken, but if articulated would have considered George a little crazy. 'And where are we going to get the thatcher?'

'I met a guy up the mountain who showed me how to do it,' said George, 'I think I got the hang of it, and he can always help out if we need help.'

'Do you mean one of them hippies?' Cornelius had asked. To the locals such as Cornelius the invasion of the great unwashed new-agers was something to be tolerated but not taken seriously. The idea that one of them would know how to build a thatched roof was incredible.

George had explained that they were not all layabouts, smoking dope and living on the dole drawn every Thursday from the post offices in Dunmanway or Bantry or Skibbereen. While the hippies were regarded with suspicion by some, they were tolerated in a benign sort of way because they were no threat and added a little colour. They weren't people with new ideas or economic solutions, and, if they had, they were bound to be hair-brained, half-cocked, crack-potted and in the long run would be left by the wayside and remain as a footnote. And yet one of their number had learnt the ancient craft of thatching, lost to the locals.

The hippies for their part regarded the locals as narrow-minded, grasping, unsophisticated philistines, destroying the very thing that made them unique and attractive: their culture and their magnificent, unspoiled landscape.

But Cornelius thought George was different. And took him more seriously. He was Irish because his parents were. He had told Cornelius a little about his background although somewhat vague on the subject. He was born in southern California, his mother had him adopted by a childless American couple, and she went back to Ireland. One of his adoptive parents died soon after, leaving George to be raised on the fringes of L.A. out in the high desert by a colourful character whom he called his uncle Sam. His real parents had left him behind for a reason that wasn't clear. His uncle, Sam Conklin had explained to him that they were both young Irish folk who had touched down in the Southland for a few years and had then gone their separate ways and somehow George had been left behind in the upheaval of their parting. He believed his natural parents were over here in Ireland somewhere, though who or where they were he didn't know. West Cork was his only reference point. He hoped that destiny would take him in the right direction and some day they might meet again.

And so he was accepted by Cornelius at face value, and liked for his straight-talking, yet sophisticated way of looking at the world. Besides, Cornelius had a sneaking regard for all things American and knew that it was a second home and a new frontier for many thousands who had left this area in the bad old days. And so the bond was strong. One thing Cornelius was sure about: Americans were friendly, courageous, and good-humoured: very different to the stiff-lipped, toffee-nosed British, Dutch and German who had also ridden in on the crest of an economic European boom thirty years before and grabbed the best sites and sea views for themselves.

They were finishing the stairs inside today. Block walls were risen and plastered outside. The basic structure completed. The hipped roof hammered with rafter and joist. Wall plates in place, batten and felt, bargeboard, soffit and fascia. There would be no gutters because none could be attached to the end of the reed. Rainwater would simply drip onto the footpath and be collected by an underground pipe running all around the house. They anticipated a few problems with getting the reed around the front of the chimney and Cornelius had devised a type of stepped, plastered apron that would merge in with the flashing and hopefully prevent any leaks when the job was done.

They were waiting for the large, round bales of reed to be delivered and these were due in a couple of days. They would come by truck, rolled on and off all the way from Turkey. This was one regret for George. Native Irish reed was becoming scarce and expensive. The variety from the southern shores of the Black Sea was cheaper and more plentiful, and, many said, more

durable. It would be delivered into Cork harbour by a
boat from Istanbul and brought down by a local trucking
company.

Inside, Cornelius's *chef d'oeuvre* was the enormous
open-hearthed chimney that soared in white, plastered
steps, uninterrupted to the roof ridge. It took George's
breath away every time he stepped inside the half-door.
Cornelius was quietly proud of his creation: 'She's a
beauty alright I suppose,' he said modestly but glowed
inwardly with quiet satisfaction, and his broad, dark-
vowelled, speech washed through the building and out
into the steady air, like a melody played on a single cello,
that George could listen to, drown in all day long and
never tire of its poetic cadence.

'That chimney reminds me of something by Gaudi.'

'Who?' asked Cornelius.

'Gaudi, he was a Spanish architect. He designed La
Sagrada Famillia.'

'La what?'

'La Sagrada Famillia, The Sacred Family. It's a famous
cathedral in Barcelona that they've been building nearly
a hundred years. It's got an amazing design, all loops and
spirals and waves. Like your chimney. No hard edges.'

Cornelius said with a droll grin: 'By God, I hope
twon't take us that long to finish the thatching.'

'And I bet you never expected to be compared to a
world-famous architect.' said George. Cornelius
laughed, mighty pleased, and then fell to wondering how
this young fellow had such an easy and familiar
knowledge of far-flung places and exotic things.
Cornelius knew a circumscribed and close-bound border

of land and if he'd been to Cork city it was a far as he
had been. The changing pace of life since he was born
had been too fast for him. Most of it had passed him by.
As they hammered the newel post, balusters and
stringers of the staircase into position Cornelius said:
'And tell me, what's it like in California?'

George described the landscape of his childhood, a
landscape that became more fantastical and more
imagined for Cornelius in the telling by the young man.
It never rained in Southern California except in January.
The sun shone all the time and there were coyotes and
raccoons and eagles in the high San Gabriel mountains
that formed a ring around Los Angeles. Through these
mountains George had hiked and cycled as a boy.
Northward were the endless vistas of the San Joaquin
valley stretching four hundred miles to Sacramento and
San Francisco. To the northeast were the mighty Sierra
Nevadas running like a spinal column the length of the
great state; due east was the high Mojave desert and
further east the low Colorado.

His uncle Sam's house was well out of L.A. halfway
into the Mojave. Nights were full of crickets' song; days
in May and June were sun-drenched and lazy, smelling of
oranges and lemons. Winter days were warm and clear,
with a particular scent of jacaranda and bougainvillea
that filled George with an aching for something he
could not describe but that took him back instantly to
when he was three or four. Some days Sam would get
restless and knock on his bedroom door at seven in the
morning. One day it would be, 'Say, George, you wanna

go to Newport beach today?' Another day it would be.
'Say, George, you wanna go to Vegas or up to Santa
Barbara?' His uncle Sam was exuberant, especially at
seven in the morning. He had big ideas. He had a new
idea for every day of the week.

'You wanna know what my plan of campaign is?' he
would ask.

'For today?'

'No, no, no, for the year. Two plays, two screenplays
and one novel.'

'That's quite a lot,' George would reply.

'Two plays, two screenplays and one novel,' Sam
would insist as if he'd already written them. He was a
big, shambling man, broad of shoulder and had a kind
heart. Yet he couldn't seem to get things together. He
knew everybody and had the lowdown on everybody but
nobody seemed to know him. He had books on
everything connected with the film industry: The Blue
Book, The Screenwriters Directory, The Screen
Director's Directory. He had Variety, The Hollywood
Reporter, he had computers with hard discs and soft
discs and modems and access to databanks of all kinds.

And now he was going to retire from the Los Angeles
Water and Power department where he had worked as a
civil servant for the past thirty years and his life was
going to begin. He had to put it on hold several times
before. First when he rescued young George off the
streets of Santa Monica and secondly when his wife
died. He was sixty and he was going to start over. He had
it all set up. No more bus rides on the freeway into the
heart of downtown every day. No more flying a desk in

some airless office with a hundred other weary workers, no more Sam do this or Sam do that. No more jibes from insolent blacks or Mexicans or Chinese. And he would have it all, realize his dreams, become a big film writer at Universal or Fox with his own parking spot, his own office and expense account; lots of power and the pick of any aspiring starlet of his choice. But the next day it would be driving to the local supermarket to bring back beans and hot coffee in a plastic cup. And so the years went by and he faithfully supervised young George's education in Simi Valley High. It was a pleasant childhood, though filled with wondering as he grew older who his real parents were? When Sam eventually told him his mother and father were Irish, George knew someday he'd set out to find his past, say goodbye to Sam.

Some days they drove through the beautiful Ventura valley along route 126. Old biplanes from a nearby airfield trundled across the lazy, morning sky, blue as the Virgin's mantle. They passed romantic barns crouched in the shade of great, spreading Holm oaks, and rich, green orange groves, with fruit drooping low in yellow abundance. Other days they drove right across L.A. to Orange County, a long drive from where they lived, probably a hundred miles, all one vast conurbation. On huge, five and six-lane freeways, swooping and diving and crisscrossing the landscape like a snakes and ladders grid game. George liked the freeways. You'd get a buzz out on them. They called them freeways because no tolls were paid on them like on the turnpikes and thruways of the east coast of America. But the name also conveyed a

sense of freedom, a sense of adventure, a journey towards
endless possibilities. It was hard for him to describe it to
Cornelius. On the freeway you feel just right. Time
seems to stand still. You are cocooned in your car in your
own little world and yet surrounded. Like a flotilla of
boats on the water the cars sweep around you, left and
right, front and rear. It is like an opera out on the
turnpike as Bruce Springsteen sang.

Other days they headed east into the desert, four
thousand feet up near Joshua Tree National Park. The
desert was beautiful at dawn, at noon, at dusk. George
remembered one morning coming up a ridge as the
shadow land gave up its secrets in the bright ring of
morning. All a warm, grey sagebrush, blackbrush, green
juniper, small-leaved creosote. And then, looming out of
the mist the peculiar Joshua Tree with its three or four-
elbowed branches bent skyward like a penitent praying.
Then at the top of the ridge, the brightest, reddest
sunburst, shooting long fingers of light along the
undersides of the mackerel clouds. As the sun rose, all
the granite rocks, all the squat, round cholla plants and
the towering distant San Jacinto mountains leaped into
view and seemed to come alive and stride before their
eyes in that wholly magical and divine dawn. The air
smelt pure as diamonds, great monuments of rock shaped
like cathedrals and elephants and skulls lay all around as
if scattered by some giant Neanderthal sowing seeds.
The rocks sat out here aeon after aeon and watched the
birds of the west: kestrels, wrens, roadrunners; and beasts
of the wild: coyotes, long-horned sheep and deer come
and go, roaming across the burnt desert floor to water

holes and escarpments, foraging for food with tiny
kangaroo rats and other more sinister two-legged
creatures in search of gold.

As his uncle Sam said it was always a shock to find
that somebody had got to someplace before you. Not
only that, but they had stumbled upon it a hundred years
before. Here in Joshua Tree there were Irish miners
working in the 1850's. Running from the Great Hunger
back home in the old country. One poor unfortunate,
Matt Riley tried to walk across the baking Pinto Basin
one fatal day only to perish from thirst a hundred yards
from the oasis at Cottonwood Springs. And there were
the outlaw McHaney brothers rustling cattle from the
Desert Queen Ranch, and the desperado Johnny Lang
who was shot in the back in a dispute over gold at the
Lost Horse Mine. Tragedy followed the Irish. Fortune
too.

Sam would explain to the youthful George that such
are the ways of man. He'd spend years trying to find a
piece of shiny metal, constructing elaborate mines of
wood and steel and wire; and then leave the entire
haphazard mess behind when the dream was over or
crushed or fading. Or when someone got too greedy and
shot his partner in the back, unable to share the spoils
with anybody after slaving so hard and long in this hot
and lonely wonderland of rocks. Greed gets in the soul,
compassion and love of neighbour are forgotten, because
man cannot bear to think he may have been tossed
down here for no reason, casually and not even by some
monster hand, with nothing which might explain to his
tortured soul who he was, where he came from, where he

was bound. *Où sommes nous? Où allons nous?* His uncle
Sam taught him a lot. He was an educated man. A good
man.

From atop the San Jacinto range they could see as far
as Mexico to the south, the San Andreas fault to the
north. They looked west but all they could see was
brown smog hiding the appalling zone: the so-called,
Inland Empire and the unspeakable wastelands of the
Cities of Industry and Commerce: cities of death and
decay where the urban sprawl was out of control; where
green fields, desert, mountain foothills, were falling
before the inevitable concrete. And he got the strongest
feeling that this beautiful landscape was ultimately
doomed by developers or doomed after the inevitable
earthquake had flattened every jerry-built warehouse,
gas station and mini mall. Soon the brown would creep
in, the water dry up and the rivers run to mud under the
scratching growl of the huge John Deere earthmovers.
Greed would destroy it. Soon only doors would flap open
in the hot desert winds waving at ghosts in ruined houses
and all this dreadful Inland Empire would return into
sand.

And as they looked eastward to Arizona try as they
might they could not discern Arcosanti, the city of the
future being built in the desert by Soleri, an Italian
architect where new-agers with dreams of a utopian
future laboured to create heaven on earth. Where
communities could flourish without cars or freeways or
smog and great open spaces would be preserved for
agriculture and recreation and nature's own favourites.
And he and his faithful uncle Sam felt a little sad that

the new city and its tubular bells was lost to all time and place, and so they moved on again, two pilgrims heading west for Idylwild.

'Well, you had a good man to bring you up,' said Cornelius, 'you were lucky.'

'I was, and I miss him,' said George, 'and I'll go back to see him one of these days when my mission is accomplished here.'

'And California sounds like a mighty fine place,' added Cornelius, 'we could do with some of that sunshine around here.'

'But I wouldn't like what has happened there to happen here,' said George, 'that would break my heart.' Cornelius nodded and thought maybe these new-age hippies weren't so crazy after all? Maybe they had a point? Although a freeway would be mighty handy to by-pass the town of Skibbereen every morning as he drove up the hills to George at the foot of Owen mountain. The bloody traffic was fierce in town. When Cornelius said this George laughed loud and long and clapped him on the back and said. 'You know Cornelius, you're a national treasure. Yourself and my uncle Sam should team up together. You'd be a right pair.'

'I suppose you'd call us the odd couple' said Cornelius with a droll laugh and settled his cap at a rakish angle on his head, 'but he knows a lot more about the modems than me. I couldn't make head nor tail of them modems.'

The truck arrived two days later with an enormous load of bales and had considerable difficulty negotiating the narrow road up to the farmyard. Eventually it could go no further and hung high at a bad turn over a beetling cliff that commanded a   panoramic view to the northwest over the Sheha mountain, the Lakes of Inchigeela, and to the southwest over Cape Clear, the Fastnet Rock, and Carberey's Hundred Isles.

'That's as far as she'll go,' said the frustrated driver. 'Nobody told me I'd have to come up this high.'

'Don't panic,' said Cornelius, 'leave it to the Yank.'

Soon George had enlisted the support of a neighbouring farmer who had sold him the old farmyard and with the help of a tractor and a front-loader with a fork they huffed and puffed the bales off the back of the truck and onto the tines of the loader. An hour later the bales were stashed, row on row in front of the cottage, ready to be stripped. The previous day George and Cornelius had erected the scaffolding and had fixed the battens to the rafters to prevent materials falling through. They had also put up the tilting fillet at the eave and gable to start the roof off at the right angle and to ensure they had the correct tension.

Then it was onto laying the first coat, starting at the eave wadd with the bottle tied at the small end. And then the brow course. While George held the sways in with spraggers to each rafter Cornelius prepared yealms of long reed and handed them up to George. 'Make sure you dress the butts on the spot board,' said George, 'they have to be combed out nice and neat, otherwise we'll have an undulating roof.'

'As long as I'm on the road,' said Cornelius, 'I never knew you had to start at the bottom and work up with thatching.'

'There you are,' said George.

As the first course was laid and the reed slowly and painstakingly crept up the roof Cornelius began to admire George more: 'Isn't it a fright that we had to wait for a young lad from America to come over here and show us how to thatch a house.'

'A lot of things have been lost,' said George, 'people seem to think that certain customs and trades are dispensable, but they're not. They're like a language, or a species facing extinction. Extinction is forever.'

And so the work continued on through the end of September and the equinoxal weather passed over. October was bright and blue and calm. And life was good. The purple loosestrife was still in bloom but fading, the evening primrose on the wane. Gone was the ladyfinger and the lesser celandine. George thatched in vertical stelches up the roof and there was the constant thud of the legget as he hit the end of the reed, pushing it into place. Soon they were up near the ridge and George had fixed a biddle into the thatch instead of a ladder to enable him to work on the higher reaches of the roof as they rose. This was the tricky part. Getting nitches of reed over the nib of the eyebrow window was slow and painstaking.

'Here's where you have to be careful,' said George. 'Because the nib is flat the rainwater is likelier to penetrate here first. And also through the ridge.' Then they placed the hazel liggers on the outside surface of the ridge at the saddle and painstakingly cut the ridge-yealm into a herring-bone shape along the apex of the roof and bound it into the main stelch with spars split from gadds of hazelnut. By late October the days were drawing in. Their work was nearly done. The hunter's moon shone down on Owen mountain.

Soon word spread through the countryside that there was a thing of beauty, a work of art to behold and every afternoon the children from the neighbouring farms came up the hillside with their curious, barking dogs to behold Cornelius's and George's masterpiece. To the new-agers it was a source of satisfaction and a cenotaph to their values of conservation and good management. Although George didn't count himself exactly among their number he appreciated their support. To the locals it was a curiosity that might have originated in a different culture rather than from their own, native, long-lost art. An art cast away and discarded in shame like their language, representing poverty and penury.

'But what about insurance?' Jim Keohane, the inquisitive publican asked when he came up to see it, 'what if it goes on fire?'

'But why should it?' George replied, 'the problem with people nowadays is they've fallen for the insurance companies' propaganda. They feed on fear so they can make larger profits from gullible people.'

'But that roof could go on fire easier surely?'

'No easier than slate roofs. You see we have a scraw laid on the rafter as a substrate for the thatch and this works like an insulation and prevents flames catching hold.'

But there were rumblings of discontent from other quarters. Certain parties, Joey Harrison among them, seemed unable to accept that this beautiful construction could serve any useful function other than as a monument to the vanity of interloping foreigners and the locals were damned if they were going to be dictated to and have their own development stopped. This was the tip of the iceberg. What was going to be next?

CHAPTER 6

*nothing to fear but
everything to lose*

Bill Cassidy stood alone in the cold reception room of a
seedy old municipal Dublin building, waiting for the
Tribunal to begin. The room had high ceilings, elaborate
cornices and centre roses; long, brown leather armchairs,
a Persian carpet and a smoothly polished mahogany
table, with a coffee urn, cups and saucers. There were
some tired old portraits on the walls but in
circumstances such as these there could have been a
galaxy of Picassos on view and he wouldn't have been
able to concentrate on them. He'd been let into the grim
old fortress of a building by a dotty-looking secretary
with horn-rimmed glasses and clipped hair, and wearing
some kind of shapeless outfit that made her look like a
defrocked nun. She appeared like the sort of person that
if her bosses asked her to swim naked across the Liffey on

Christmas Day she would do it without a murmur. Not that anybody would be watching. He didn't sit down. He never did in these Gulag-like places lest his bones would atrophy and he'd never rise again. He looked idly around. It was the smell that struck you first. Was it urine or rising damp? The former he would wager. How could people stand it day in day out, working away at dusty documents, staring through the tired Georgian windows at the rain? The dead hand of bureaucracy pervaded everywhere. It would take an enormous burst of energy for someone trapped in the clutches of this spider web of mediocrity to launch themselves into the orbit of another career. Few ever did.

It was the feeling of lack of control that always got to Bill. You spent your life working towards something, building with blood sweat and tears, only for some state-appointed bureaucrat with a chip on both shoulders to attempt to wrest everything away from you based on the flimsiest of conceits.

He had to meet his legal team earlier and he'd been walking around the gloomy corridors of the Four Courts in the stale, wet heart of Dublin, the cast of a fishing line from the Liffey. What a grim, cheerless river it was, with a cold wind forever blowing down it; always struck him as he walked over it. When the tide was out it looked like a dirty stream enclosed behind high, fortress-like walls. Full tide was an improvement but there was something about its mean and narrow aspect that reflected in many ways the personality of its denizens. Maybe Joyce had it just about right. On the whole. *Anna Livia plurabelle* indeed. Other cities like Paris or London had wide, romantic rivers with great embankments and promenades, communities of barge people living on colourful craft, river cruisers constantly plying under beautiful bridges. The Shannon was broad and majestic. Even Cork's lovely Lee was a more noble, twisting, more adventurous river.

Perhaps it was the way he was feeling. Summoned here peremptorily to give evidence at a Tribunal inquiring into how he'd made his money. It was a module relating to money laundering and the disposal of criminal assets. Bill had to sit waiting for ludicrously pompous lawyers in straggling wigs and schoolmasters gowns. The longer he stayed the more he felt himself on the set of one of those satirical films made by Monty Python some years ago. This place was like a depressing beehive buzzing with large-bellied, unfit-looking barristers shuffling around making crude, snorting noises through their nostrils. Flouncing around in gowns. And there were always solicitors puffing along behind them, frowning too much, as if their particular burden of responsibility was far greater and more important than that of most other mortals. Why couldn't they relax for goodness sake? What were they after all but mere administrators doing a job that didn't require any great skill or genius? Of course most were secretly aware of the inconsequence of their occupations. If fifty percent of the lawyers in the country were wiped out it wouldn't make the slightest difference to the well-being of everybody in general. Lawyers were like auctioneers: the work they did expanded to feed their numbers. Film crews and journalists too for that matter. But had any one of them ever found a cure for cancer; sent a satellite through the rings of Saturn; composed a symphony to lift up the hearts of men or written a great, enduring novel to chronicle that men had bestrode the earth. Or built a Channel tunnel?

But they were cunning. They always served you with a motion on the Friday before the holidays to make sure your vacation was properly loused up, and then when the day of your appointed appearance before the Tribunal arrived you were kept waiting for as long as possible to make sure you were properly stewed by the time you were ushered in before the long, high table.

Where did power truly lie? Which institution had a monopoly on it? On his way here he'd driven as far as the outskirts and then walked through the centre of Dublin. Something which he liked to do occasionally to change his way of thinking if he was in a rut. The enormous burgeoning University College Dublin was a complete world of youth existing almost like an alien colony on the face of a distant planet, where the power of the future was formed. Not far away across the motorway from the groves of academe was that self-sustaining, self-important institution, RTE, the television and radio station which along with the print media was at the cutting edge in the formation of the country's opinions and mores, having assumed a mantle long since abandoned by the Church. Then on to the bustling hospitals where doctors often played God with people who had no choice but to forget the profit and loss, because other more immediate considerations were staring them in the face; like death and decay; and the prospects for their children without them. There certainly was power there. Sceptre and crown must tumble down.

Onward to Dáil Éireann where politicians held nominal power but whose main preoccupation was to get themselves elected next time round and so the requirement to be nice to everybody was paramount. What about the bankers who managed the money, the priests who comforted the dying, the farmers who ploughed the fields and scattered the good seed on the land? Or the swashbuckling carpenters, electricians, bricklayers and plumbers? What happened if they pulled the plug? The policemen, the army: what onslaught could they withstand? Who was driving the country now? Was it entrepreneurs like himself, Bill Cassidy, who took big risks, thought up imaginative, creative projects, who took on and beat the best in the outside world? He'd read somewhere that the great societies, Egypt, Greece, Rome reached their full flowering when the artists and creators were in the ascendant. As soon as the blockers took over the downhill slide began. And these were the army, the bureaucrats and the lawyers. The lawyers who were supposed to facilitate contract-makers and project-builders but who, in his experience, scuppered with their hubris more deals than they assisted.

He got a gentle nudge on his arm from his concerned Counsel sitting beside him. The Chairman had asked him a question and in his daydream he'd been lulled into another world and never even noticed that the droning Counsel for the Tribunal had finished his interminable and stultifying opening speech. Besides, the heat was so high coming from the coughing radiators, and the windows so tightly closed and there were so many barristers crammed into the place it felt like the black hole of Calcutta.

'Mr. Cassidy, do you wish to make a response to the opening statement of Mr. Carter?' The Chairman had a pleasant face and kindly eyes that were perhaps a little intimidated by the legal arsenal Bill had mustered. What was his name, Huggins? Odd name too. Had he a weak face? Wasn't there something porcelain about the way it was put together? Almost pretty. Bill suspected it would fracture easily. How'd he get this job? Safe upstairs. Hide out from the big, bad world and join the golf club. But not the worst of them by a long chalk.

Bill consulted with his Counsel and decided to let the hound of heaven loose. Why bark if you kept dogs?

David J. Cantwell got to his feet and pushed his jaw upwards as he adjusted the starched collar below his Adam's apple and decided to take these proceedings by the scruff of the neck. Cantwell was a very tall, thin man, with a long, dark, saturnine, Norman face and quite thick lips upon which a ghost of a smile continually played. The coincidence of his name and appearance with that of a certain doughty, eight-hundred year old knight who reposed on a plinth in a church in Kilkenny, with long legs akimbo, had earned him the nickname of Cantwell *Fada* among his peers in the Law Library. The eyes were blue and humorous below a high, domed forehead and what scant hair he had left was thinning fast off that great dome, and completely gone in the round spot above his poll.

Cantwell had the expression of a man who finds the entire panoply of human activity one vast comedy from which he would prefer to be detached but with which he reluctantly has to engage. He gave the impression that he'd prefer to be pruning his roses or singing Gregorian Chant rather than arguing in a sweaty courtroom. But such was Cantwell's vast discipline and learning, and his love of winning, that the effort was continuously worth the candle. He was also rather fond of money, *"he had a very special love of gold,"* like the doctor in Chaucer's *Canterbury Tales* and the size of his fee was commensurate with the size of his brain. Bill didn't mind paying it. Cantwell was one of the few barristers whose company he hugely enjoyed, and who rarely lost a case from a standing start. The contrast between Cantwell and Carter, the chief counsel for the Tribunal couldn't have been more marked. Carter was small, demure-looking with an undistinguished face except for a very prominent, hooked, Roman nose. His personality was dull as Cantwell's was flamboyant. But sitting beside Carter was mettle more attractive: his colleague, Martha Williams was a tall, female barrister with a wide, mobile mouth. She had a strong aquiline nose and the impression her face conveyed was of strength and self-containment in contrast to her colleague whose face was rather weak. Her brown hair was streaked in blonde highlights and cut in a peek-a-boo style just to the nape of her neck. Her big eyes were somewhere between hazel and green. They had a mesmeric quality that could quickly change from cold to humorous and back again. Overall she had a beautiful, secretive, cruel, self-absorbed face. She exuded confidence and intelligence but the initial impression was of a coiled sexual energy that she appeared to be quite conscious of. What was she doing here? Bill wondered. When would they let her slip the leash?

'Mr. Carter,' said Cantwell, 'we've been sitting here listening to your rambling account of my client's impressive list of assets and you have succeeded in telling us absolutely nothing that we don't already know, and that's not already in the public domain. My client's assets and his liabilities are an open book: registered in Land Registry folios, Companies Office Share Registers and extensive bank statements. Copies of everything have already been furnished to the Tribunal. My client is guilty of nothing. However, you yourself are guilty of something far more unforgivable and it is this.' Cantwell paused for emphasis, looked down at his papers and then fixed his eye on the topmost further corner of the darkly lit old hearing room and continued: 'You have committed the egregious offence of putting us all to sleep.' A hoot of snickering laughter went round the room and even the Chairman high on his bench permitted himself an amused chuckle. The female barrister's eyes fairly danced with suppressed mirth.

'Now your worship,' went on Cantwell in exaggerated deference to the Chairman, 'if the only transgression on Mr. Cassidy's part that my friend can point to is to have accumulated a very impressive schedule of assets, I am sorry but that is no reason to drag him before this Tribunal and in the process put his reputation in serious jeopardy. I am not denying that it may instil pangs of envy or even jealousy in the hearts of the man or woman on the street, or indeed among the distinguished members of the legal and media profession in this room, but it is not a crime. That my client is a very wealthy man is undeniable but it is no sin. That he started out in life from a position of deprivation and disadvantage and propelled himself through dint of talent and industry into the front rank of Ireland's rich list is also undeniable. But he is not alone. In the Ireland of today there are many like him. I could name at least fifty other Irishmen, contemporaries of my client, who have ridden to great success on the crest of a wave of affluence that has swept over this country in the past ten years. These people are household names. Indeed, Mr. Chairman, you have already had the pleasure of the company of several such individuals who shall remain nameless here today, but who, alas, have already been named and vilified in the media and who have been powerless to prevent it. Becoming rich is not a crime. It is only a crime to do so by illegal means. Your counsel, Mr. Chairman, in his opening statement has demonstrated no illegality on my client's part. Nothing so much as a misdemeanour has been adverted to here today. And indeed Mr. Chairman, unless your Counsel can dredge up something considerably more substantial, then I shall have to ask you to abandon this witch-hunt against my client and allow him to go about his business.'

The Chairman nodded politely and allowed himself the merest of smiles as he considered Cantwell's assertion. 'Well, Mr. Cantwell, you have quite rightly pointed out that your client is guilty of no crime, but neither is this Tribunal making such a case. Our remit is to investigate certain dealings on your client's part which may or may not establish that he acted wrongfully. And I stress the words may or may not. Our function is not to find your client guilty of a crime. That is not within our power. It is to make certain findings based on the evidence adduced before us and then to make recommendations. Once we have your client's co-operation he has nothing to fear from us.'

'Nothing to fear my lord, but everything to lose,' said Cantwell. 'The fact is that a man may be destroyed by your Tribunal without ever being charged with a crime before a court of law. Hardly a satisfactory situation from an ethical point of view.'

'I did not establish the Tribunals, Mr. Cantwell. The Oireachtas did that as you well know. My job is to oversee the work as dictated by the legislators and keep within the established parameters. Now, can we move along here, Mr. Carter?'

Carter stood and bowed obsequiously to the Chairman and said: 'Thank you, Chairman. As my friend has rightly pointed out I have made my opening statement and I am sorry for putting him to sleep in the process. Bearing that in mind and at the risk of reoffending I am now handing the second part of this examination over to my esteemed colleague, Ms Martha Williams whom I trust will have a more positive impact on my friend's state of alertness. We now propose to question Mr. Cassidy directly and perhaps he'd be good enough to take the stand.'

As Bill was standing to go up to the witness box, Cantwell half rose to his feet and whispered from behind his open hand into Bill's ear: '*Prends garde a toi avec cette femme.*' Bill frowned, then nodded and walked to the witness box and was sworn in by a clerk: 'I swear by Almighty God that I will tell the truth, the whole truth and nothing but the truth.'

Bill was dressed in one of his sharpest dark pinstripe suits, white Charvet shirt, red, silk tie. He presented a formidable sight. The epitome of the successful white male. He sat confidently in his chair and waited for the vixen to begin.

Martha Williams turned the full glare of her luminous headlights on Bill Cassidy. Her look was cool, brazen, unintimidated. Bill's look was one of slightly detached bemusement. He had dealt with international bankers, hard-nosed Hollywood producers, wily pin-hookers buying and selling thoroughbreds, ruthless industrialists, entrepreneurs and gamblers who would fleece you in the blinking of an eye and laugh in your face. What did this one think she could throw at him that he hadn't seen before a hundred times? Still the view was attractive: decolletage a little deep for these hallowed halls? Was she wearing fishnet stockings underneath that funereal gown? Perish the thought. No peruke today? Not obliged to wear the horsehair in these proceedings. She certainly looked her best with that glossy, shining, mane. Just his type of filly. Whoa there. Stirrings in the loins. Not here? Impossible yet true. He blinked and tried to focus. Had she noticed? If so it was a bad start. Martha coiled an expensive black pen between her index and middle fingers and Bill could smell her perfume from ten feet away. It wafted pleasurably over him like petals from blown roses on the grass. What was that French phrase Cantwell used? Watch out?

'Mr. Cassidy,' began Martha, 'you're a married man?'

'Yes.'

'But, you're separated.'

'Yes,' said Bill.

'Not divorced?'

'No.'

What kind of an opening was this? Unorthodox to say the least. He looked quickly towards Cantwell, who was on his feet in a shot. 'Really, Mr. Chairman,' he deplored, 'what relevance my client's marital status has to the matters at hand is difficult to see?'

'It is relevant,' said Martha, 'in the context of clarifying the exact nature and extent of Mr. Cassidy's holdings.'

'You may continue,' said the Chairman.

'You list a villa in the south of France in a town called Grasse.'

'Yes,' smiled Bill and added ruefully, 'it's the perfume capital of the world I believe.'

'And your wife lives there?'

'Most of the time.'

'Lucky her, I must ask her to get me a bottle of Fragonard next time she's coming home.'

'I'm sure she'd be happy to, ' said Bill, 'but my nose tells me you already have an adequate supply.'

Martha paused, perhaps secretly pleased and said: 'And you bought this property for her?'

'Yes, as part of the terms of our separation she got that house as well as a townhouse in Ballsbridge.'

'Where in Ballsbridge?'

'Raglan Road.'

'How apt,' exclaimed Martha with a kind of sarcastic chortle, 'and presumably you now rue the day her dark hair ensnared you?' A titter of suppressed laughter flitted around the courtroom. Reporters got busy with their notepads. This had the makings of an interesting encounter in the midst of the usual deadly dull goings-on at these Tribunals. Bill considered the observation: 'Not really, my wife is a fair woman, we'd raised our children, there was enough to go round for everybody. I'd be much more concerned at being ensnared by you.'

There were loud hollers of laughter from the assembled rubberneckers. The dotty-looking secretary-stenographer didn't know where to look. Cantwell gave a dry smirk.

'*Touché*, Mr. Cassidy,' said Martha and examined the nail polish on the fingernails on her left hand.

'Really, Mr. Chairman,' said Cantwell, on his feet again, 'this is all very droll I'm sure but where is it leading us? Have we been summoned here simply to amuse the masses?'

'You'll see soon enough where we're going, Mr. Cantwell,' said Martha Williams, 'you must be patient. I'm sure your client is. And complex too.'

'This is not a psycho-analysis session, Ms Williams, this is a legal Tribunal,' said an exasperated Cantwell.

'Please get to the point Ms. Williams,' urged the Chairman.

Martha shifted on her feet and scratched under an armpit. Bill regarded her with an ironic but guarded demeanour. Was she flirting with him or trying to distract him? Take no chances.

'Are you aware,' she continued, 'of the many rumours circulating about you, I mean the speculation on the source of your wealth?'

'I read the papers occasionally,' said Bill, 'but that's just what it is, pure speculation.'

'You're quite the mystery man aren't you, Mr. Cassidy. You've travelled the world, lived in America, you own yachts and racehorses.'

'That's no big deal nowadays,' said Bill, 'I'm afraid the reality is rather more mundane than the picture newspapers paint.'

'Precisely the point, Mr.Cassidy,' cut in Martha, 'you see there are certain things about you that don't quite...stack up as it were.'

'Such as?'

'In your elaborate and extensive affidavit to this Tribunal setting out the history of your holdings and wealth, you state you were born on a farm in County Cork.'

'Yes I was,' said Bill, 'what's wrong with that?'

'How did a poor farmer's son make the quantum leap from being penniless in the late seventies to being an extremely wealthy man today?'

'You mustn't be reading those tabloid newspapers that you seem to love so much if you think I'm the only poor boy to have made a fortune in Ireland today.' said Bill deftly.

'But there are gaps in the progression, the dots don't connect. What's your secret?'

'That's what everyone asks a successful businessman, Ms. Williams, but I'm afraid it can't be taught. It's an art. If it was easy everyone would be living in a mansion in Beverly Hills.'

'Really, Mr. Cassidy,' said Martha, her brow furling and her eyes widening.

'Really and truly,' said Bill evenly, 'it requires great nerves, taking risks, lateral thinking. Above all thinking big.'

'And you learned how to do all this on your own? You don't list any third-level education on your curriculum vitae, no MBA's.'

'The secret of my success can't be taught in a college,' said Bill, 'any amount of law degrees won't make you seriously rich.'

'Are you impugning my profession, Mr. Cassidy?' asked Martha brightly.

'On the contrary,' laughed Bill, 'some of my best friends are lawyers.'

'Quite,' said Martha with a peeved expression. 'If I may move on. Did you know a man named Frank Russell?'

'I did,' said Bill, 'he was a good friend, but he's dead, sadly.'

'Wild Frank, I believe he was called. Tell me, was he one of your mentors?'

'Mentor might be a bit strong. But he did teach me a thing or two.'

'Such as?'

'He taught me not to be too deferential to people like you,' said Bill with a smile.

'Did he also teach you how to launder millions through racetracks and hotels?'

'I don't know what you mean,' said Bill.

'You own a hotel near Kinsale, Mr. Cassidy, a very luxurious hotel?'

'Yes I do,'

'You have many international businessmen staying there?'

'Japanese mainly, they like to play golf.'

'And movie stars?'

'Those too.'

'And people with connections to organized crime and paramilitary organizations?'

'I'm afraid I've never met any of those,' said Bill.

'Oh, really, Mr. Cassidy,' said Martha, warming to her subject, 'you come from a Republican background don't you?'

'Who told you that?'

'We have ways and means of finding out such things.' Was she threatening him? Bill shifted in his seat and looked to Cantwell who shrugged and motioned him to answer.

'Do you come from a Republican background, Mr. Cassidy?' repeated Martha.

'I do,' said Bill, 'so what?'

'Are you proud of it?'

'I have no feelings about it one way or the other. I have no control over accidents of birth. My father fought for Irish Independence with half the young men of his age in Ireland of that era.'

'You've heard the expression die-hard?'

'I have.'

'Your father was a die-hard was he not?'

'In what sense?'

'He supported Sinn Fein and the old IRA.'

'Yes, but I really think you're barking up the wrong tree here. What my father did as a young man has no bearing on what I did as a young man. There is no similarity or comparison between my life and my father's life. It's like we were born on two different planets.'

'Except it could make you a secret sympathiser and facilitator for paramilitary organizations to launder their ill-gotten gains through your hotels.'

'Objection, objection, Mr. Chairman, this is absurd,' interrupted Cantwell, shouting above the murmurs and whisperings of the onlookers. Bill could only shrug and shake a disbelieving head towards Cantwell.

'And Wild Frank Russell was your go-between for years, your bagman, wasn't he, Mr. Cassidy!' Martha William's shrill soprano rose above Cantwell's deeper baritone.

'I'm afraid you'll have to ask himself that,' laughed Bill grimly. The hearing room erupted into raucous laughter.

'You covered your tracks cunningly, didn't you, Mr. Cassidy?'

The reporters were scribbling furiously. Barristers scattered around the room were whispering animatedly. David Cantwell leaped to his feet.

'Mr. Chairman, Mr. Chairman, we are entering the realms of fantasy here. Ms Williams is drawing inferences and jumping to conclusions that have no connection with Mr. Cassidy's evidence here today. She has gone from asking my client seemingly innocuous questions about his private life to suggesting he is a fellow traveller with the IRA. This is nothing short of scandalous. It is outlandish. This is just the type of wild allegation allowed in these Tribunals which is not backed up by a scintilla of evidence of any kind yet is allowed to be reported on and dressed up as being the truth to the serious detriment of my client's reputation. This is how people were treated in kangaroo courts in the old Soviet Union. It is a farce from beginning to end. Unless you produce evidence to support your sensational suggestions you must withdraw them, apologise to my client and allow him to go on his way.'

'I will produce evidence,' said Martha Williams coolly, 'but I must ask you to adjourn the proceedings, Mr. Chairman, to enable me subpoena a key witness who has been unable to attend today. On the reconvening of this Tribunal I intend to produce this witness who will not only support my contentions but will establish conclusively that there is an insidious pattern and a system which has made Mr. Cassidy a very wealthy man. The origin of Mr. Cassidy's ill-gotten gains will be exposed.'

There were shouts of support and condemnation from some members of the assembled public. Cantwell shouted to Martha Williams to immediately withdraw

her remarks under pain of censure by the Bar Council.
The Chairman banged his gavel and called for order:

'Ladies and gentlemen, can we have a modicum of
order here? Mr. Cantwell, your client will have ample
opportunity to rebut whatever evidence Ms. Williams
adduces on the next occasion when this Tribunal sits.
I'm adjourning matters now until the 10th of June and if
on that day Ms Williams cannot produce anything more
substantial than the speculation which she indulged in
here today, then I'm afraid Mr. Cassidy will be free to go.
Thank you.'

As Bill left the hearing room with Cantwell *Fada* at
his side and emerged into the dreary half-light of the
cold March afternoon they were met by a phalanx of
shouting reporters and a display of flashbulbs bright as
the Leonids meteor shower on a dark November night.
It was time for a drink and quickly too. It was about 4
o'clock as they hurried down past the Ormond Hotel
and Essex Bridge into the enveloping cloak of the
approaching twilight.

CHAPTER 7

that form endearing

'She never laid a glove on you, dear boy,' said Cantwell *Fada*, gazing absent-mindedly at the passing parade of evening pedestrians hurrying home to apartments and warm home fires on this dry, cold, March evening. Some weeks past the Ides of March. Summer time coming in on the weekend. The clocks would go forward. Civil servants, department-store workers, young barristers dressed in earnest pinstripes and waistcoats, humping their black book-bags over their shoulders: all wearing out shoe leather along the banks of the Liffey in the daily shuffle of their circumscribed lives. He'd done all that himself twenty-five years ago. Painstakingly he'd built up his practice on tedious running-down accident cases, licensing applications, conveyancing and company law motions; until now at the zenith of his glittering career he was able to command five thousand per day for showing up to defend a big wheel like Bill Cassidy; on top of a whacking forty thousand up front for merely deigning to accept the brief in the first place.

The cold outside would go through your bones. Was it his imagination or had the pattern of the prevailing wind changed in the last couple of years to a northeasterly airflow during the months of January, February and March? He must check it with that erudite Brendan McWilliams in the Weather Eye of *The Irish Times*. It must have something to do with global warming. Odd that it should be colder than normal of late at this time of year though? Where did that wind come from: Novaya Zemlya?

He was sitting opposite Bill Cassidy on a low, soft, chocolate-brown leather couch in the *nouvelle vague* surroundings of the lounge of the Morrison Hotel on Lower Ormond Quay in the heart of Dublin. He himself wasn't too keen on the strict minimalist lines of this establishment with its black and white, hard-edged furniture, and its abstract paintings but Bill told him he liked it. It seemed he owned the apartment block behind it on Jervis street and he liked to use this as a kind of downtown office. He stayed here some nights rather than drive out to the suburbs. Cantwell couldn't imagine himself doing that. Far too set in his ways. But the place did have its pluses. The seats were unusually comfortable, the cakes were excellent and the whiskey top class. They had a very large selection of the best Scotch and Irish though his preferred beverage was Jack Daniels from the hills of Tennessee. Of course the location was perfect. In the city-centre but not in the rougher part. Within walking distance of the Four Courts but far away enough to carry out discreet consultations safe from the prying eyes in that incestuous hive.

The view out the great floor-to-ceiling, ten foot high windows was panoramic. You could see all the way from the graceful Ha'penny Bridge on the left, on past Temple Bar and some interesting architectural gems such as the Sunlight Chambers across the river, festooned with mosaics of Dublin life on its outside walls: a rare Venetian treasure set down in old Viking Dublin. Then on past the Clarence Hotel beloved of Bono and the rock and roll set, and over Essex Bridge to the Ormond Hotel on this side of the river where Joyce set the famous *Sirens* scene in *Ulysses*. He'd played a part in that once in his student days at the Players Theatre in Trinity: *Blazes Boylan* was it? Anyway the fellow who's having it away with *Molly* in the afternoon. The fellow who wore the white boater.

Bill was on the mobile phone to somebody and as Cantwell sipped his Jack Daniels he was filled with a warm glow all over at the comforting thought of having been born and bred in Dublin. Flying colours all the way. Father a Fitzwilliam Square solicitor, he himself an old Gonzaga boy, trained by the Jesuits; then Arts and an LLB at Trinity and finally the King's Inns: dinners, wigs and gowns. Rugby on the weekends at Bective and Old Wesley. Triple Crown weekends at Landsdowne. What a civilized upbringing. He supposed he should count himself lucky. How he loved this city, this river, every street and back lane and Georgian square. Never really lived anywhere else. Wouldn't want to. How could you beat Rathgar and tennis on Sunday mornings?

He observed his young client across from him and didn't see a fellow traveller. Young? Why did he consider him young? Bill Cassidy was in his early fifties, nearly as old as himself, yet he seemed to come from a different, younger generation; a different country altogether. Was Bill what they called a baby boomer? He himself never understood that term. But there was something boyishly innocent about him sitting there smiling as he spoke on the phone. An enthusiasm that Cantwell himself lacked, despite his certainties. Bill was forever attached to the umbilical chord of his youth. Forever chasing elusive dreams across the landscape of his imagination. He was reminded of that character in the Fitzgerald novel, what was it...*The Great Gatsby?* Where had he first met him? Introduced by their common acquaintance the ubiquitous Wild Frank Russell in the horseshoe bar of the Shelbourne Hotel, on the pleasant pastures of St. Stephen's Green. Wild Frank's second home, and the stomping ground of every would-be millionaire, gambler, aspiring artist and mountebank whoever set foot in dear old dirty Dublin.

He began humming: *M'appari tout amor*, the signature tune from the opera, *Martha* by Flotow:

> "When first I saw that form endearing,
> Sorrow from me seemed to depart..."

Pavarotti had a very good recent rendition of it. Then the coincidence hit him like a sledgehammer: *Martha*, *the Sirens* who sang to trap unwary sailors and lure them to their deaths. The theme running through Joyce's chapter in his masterpiece. Himself: the solicitor, *Richie Goulding? Blazes Boylan:* Bill Cassidy? Martha Williams: *Martha Clifford?* The time: 4 o'clock. Almost the exact time and place. My God, it was too much. He'd better get Bill off that phone right away and tell him. Cantwell, in spite of his clear-eyed, logical mind was inordinately superstitious when it came to coincidences.

As Bill finally got off the phone he noticed that Cantwell had gone suddenly silent and had a preoccupied look of agitation on his usually urbane face. 'Everything alright, David?' he asked. Cantwell relayed to him his insights concerning Martha Williams and the *Sirens* and the place they were sitting. It was the damndest thing. Bill was vaguely impressed with Cantwell's book knowledge but didn't attach as much significance to it as his lawyer. 'You know what strikes me, David,' he said, 'sometimes you intellectuals can't separate fact from fiction, you have your heads sunk so deeply in books,'

On that note Cantwell stood and said he'd really better be going. His wife was having one of their staid old dinner parties and he'd better be sober. They'd be having a judge or two over, and a couple of chartered accountants. 'Sounds like a scintillating evening,' said Bill ironically.

'You are, of course, perfectly welcome to come over,' said Cantwell hastily, 'if you're at a loose end.'

'Thanks,' said Bill, 'but I really think I'm good for judges for one day. I'll pass if you don't mind.'

'Suit yourself dear boy,' said Cantwell almost relieved. He really did believe in bad karma. He wanted to be gone and quickly too. As they walked towards the door he asked: 'So what will you do, drive out to the suburbs I presume, have an early night?'

'Maybe, maybe not,' answered Bill, 'I may stay overnight. They usually keep a cubby hole for me here if I'm stuck. I think I'll just sink another glass or two of Claret and throw my head down here.'

'Don't you think you should go home?' said Cantwell. 'You've had a very trying day.'

'Just a lot of *sturm und drang* as they say in Germany,' said Bill.

'Oh, I agree,' said Cantwell, 'there's not very much substance in our friend's performance. But she is dissembling. We have to be careful with her.'

'I wonder who's this witness she's talking about?'

'It doesn't matter who it is,' said Cantwell, 'we'll cross that bridge when we come to it. Relax tonight and don't worry about the inevitable headlines in tomorrow's papers. It'll be a one-day wonder. The public have a very short attention span these days…but I really think you should go home tonight, no point in hanging around making it easy for those reporters.'

Bill slapped Cantwell on the shoulder and laughed. 'This *Sirens* stuff is really getting to you, isn't it. Do you believe in ghosts?'

'Do *you* believe in them, more to the point?' asked Cantwell with a look of vague alarm behind his eyes.

'Ghosts don't frighten me anymore,' said Bill, 'I've been followed by a few for several years now.'

They shook hands and Bill watched Cantwell's tall, erect figure stride away. He had a strange pointy-toed type of walk, as if picking the spot carefully before planting each step. Cantwell had few peers in the courtroom and his mind was as agile as a cat going through a skylight. Yet how would he have performed in a different arena? Bill couldn't imagine his ponderous feet coping under a high Garryowen and a yelping pack of Munstermen bearing down upon him.

When he was gone out of sight along the new boardwalk and into the firmament of the bright lights shining from O'Connell Bridge, Bill turned back inside. He went left into the dark shadows of the bar and pulled up a high stool. The odd straggler was trickling in. The barman came over and asked cheerfully: 'What can I get you, Mr. Cassidy, sir?'

'Let me see, John, let me see. How about a Dewars and ginger ale on the rocks.'

'A Dewars coming up.'

' Slow tonight,' said Bill.

'Always slow after St.Patrick's Day. Are you staying with us tonight?'

'I think I will.'

'Do you want me to reserve your usual suite, sir?'

'You're very kind, John,' said Bill, 'that would be great.'

The barman placed Bill's drink on the counter and then walked up the bar and lifted a telephone to reserve Bill's room.

It was about six-thirty in the evening and Bill was halfway through his second Scotch when Martha

Williams walked in. There were no more than a dozen
drinkers scattered around the four-sided bar and she'd
have had to be blind to miss him. She didn't. She came
towards him with a slow, deliberate, jaunty walk. Almost
in slow motion it seemed to Bill. Was the drink going to
his head? She'd changed her outfit. Gone was the
amorphous black gown and the business suit. She was
now wearing a low-cut black dress, high heels and a fur
coat. She drew abreast of him at the bar and then slowly
turned her head. An ironic smile played on her lips. He
got a whiff of her perfume as she went past him. She
smelt better than ever. Then she continued on slowly
around the bar as if looking for somebody. She again
caught his eye from across the bar and then continued
until she came full circle and stood in front of him. 'So,'
she intoned, 'we meet again Mr. Cassidy.'

'Sooner than I expected,' said Bill. She looked him up
and down and said: 'Glad to see you're still in one piece.'

'I'm glad you're glad,' he smiled, 'but I don't shatter
easily, Ms Williams.'

'I know, 'she said, 'fragile is not an adjective I'd ever
ascribe to you.'

'Nor you,' laughed Bill. She looked around the bar
and back towards Bill. 'Looking for somebody?' he asked.

'I'm due to meet a friend, we're going to the theatre.
She's late as usual.'

'What's on?' asked Bill.

'Ralph Fiennes is in something. With him it doesn't
matter what.'

'Well, let me get you a drink to warm you up for
Ralph.'

'Thanks,' she said, 'but I'm already quite warm after my encounter with you today.'

'Warm,' laughed Bill, 'you look pretty cool to me.' Martha couldn't quite contain her *sang-froid*. She laughed a deep, husky laugh.

'Well, Bill, may I call you Bill...?'

'Sure, if I may call you Martha?'

'Of course. And I'll take a drink on one condition.'

'What's that?'

'That we don't talk about today.'

'I never mix business with pleasure,' said Bill.

'Very droll, Bill. Neither do I,' said Martha, as she undraped her fur coat to reveal gleaming bare shoulders and a glittering diadem hanging around her neck and diamond earrings. Bill pulled over a high stool and she sat on it.

'What's your pleasure, or should I say what's your poison?' he asked dryly.

'You don't hate me that much do you?' She laughed again, a deep, sensuous laugh.

'On the contrary I think you're a very formidable woman.'

'You like formidable women?'

'Depends on the woman. Let's say, I like the thrill of the chase, matching wits.'

'You think I'm chasing you?' she asked cryptically.

'Not in a romantic sense. You're trying to trip me up though.' said Bill, 'but you're not quick enough.' He regarded her with a steady, slightly world-weary gaze. Then he sat on the high stool opposite her. Their knees almost touched. The barman hovered near them, not quite out of hearing, waiting for the order. She noticed and said to Bill: 'By the way it's a malt.'

'What?' asked Bill, already distracted by her aroma in spite of himself.

'The drink,' she laughed, 'it's a malt, a single malt.'

Bill turned to his friend, John, 'A single malt for the lady, John,' he said.

'Ice?' asked John as he lifted the bottle from its bracket.

'Yes,' she said. They watched the golden liquid trickling over the cold cubes, heard them crackle and hiss. The barman pushed the glass towards her and said to Bill: 'Another one, Mr. Cassidy?'

'Why not,' said Bill. The second chinking glass glided across the marble-topped bar.

'Good health,' said Bill and raised his glass.

'Good health,' smiled Martha but the ice had not quite left her eyes.

They both drank, eyeing each other warily over the tops of their glasses. After a moment Bill said: 'That's a ballsy drink, if I may say so.'

She put her glass on the bar and chose her words: 'You mean it's a ballsy drink for a woman?'

'It suits you,' he said.

'I get the impression you're not used to dealing with a woman with balls,' she said coolly.

'It's an interesting image,' he said and drank, then shuddered and blinked his eyes.

'What's the matter, Bill?' she asked with a suggestion of sarcasm.

'Someone just walked on my grave,' he said.

'Maybe you just can't handle the image of a dominant woman?'

'Dominant, yes, that's an interesting image too,' he said, 'but already you seem a lot more human than you did today.'

'It's a profession, a job. We're guns for hire. I could be on your side at another time and place. If I were on your side would you have me be any other way?'

'No, no, you're absolutely right. I wouldn't have you any other way.'

His hand accidentally touched her crossed knee for a second and then withdrew. Her leg extended long and smooth as ivory to her high-heeled shod foot. It's continuous up and down motion was the only indication that she was molten inside. He let his hand brush against her knee for another moment. She did not appear to notice but looked slowly up into his eyes. The ice had melted to a smouldering intensity. Her lips were slightly parted and her tongue rested on her lower lip. At that moment her theatre friend put her hand on her shoulder and said: 'Oh, Martha, I'm so sorry, I'm late. Traffic is terrible on the Howth Road.'

Martha said: 'Julia, I thought you'd stood me up.'

'Well, it looks as if that wouldn't have bothered you too much,' said Julia and smiled at Bill. Martha stood and straightened out her dress.

'This is Bill Cassidy,' she said, 'meet Julia Clancy.' Bill extended his hand. 'Another legal eagle I presume?' he said.

'No, as a matter of fact Julia is a doctor,' said Martha and put her coat on.

'Very nice,' said Bill, 'a couple of impressive ladies by the sound of it. Well, enjoy the theatre.'

'You're not going to join us?' asked Julia looking admiringly at him.

'Not tonight I'm afraid. I had a hard day and I've an early start.'

'Goodbye,' said Martha, 'it was nice meeting you again. And thanks for the drink.' She held out her hand. He held it for a moment slightly longer than necessary.

'A pleasure,' said Bill and continued in a low voice. 'David Cantwell warned me about you. I can't imagine why?'

She put her finger to her lips: 'Can't discuss that, remember?'

She pulled her coat around her like a protective shield. She had reverted back into a chrysalis.

Bill Cassidy tossed in troubled sleep that night in his luxury suite in the Morrison Hotel on the banks of the Liffey. His thoughts whirled in a maelstrom of sights, sounds and smells. He saw the face of David J. Cantwell looming through the mist on Essex Bridge, holding up an admonishing finger and he heard the warning words: "Beware, beware that woman." He kept seeing the image of Martha Williams' beautiful face buried deep in a pillow, her tongue extended in pleasure as she moaned 'yes, yes, oh yes,' and his hands cradling the twin mounds of her glorious behind, reared up for his delectation; her gleaming thighs spread wide. And his tortured thoughts wandered south over the lonely roads of Ireland to a little house on the Atlantic coast and an old man with a walking stick taking shelter from the storm under a hawthorn bush, with the wild waves at his feet.

When the bell-boy brought his breakfast and his newspaper in the morning the first image that registered on his drowsy brain was that of himself and Cantwell *Fada* fleeing a posse of hungry reporters outside the Tribunal headquarters, with the great, crumbling old buildings of Viking Dublin framing the picture. Behind them, with a clearly visible triumphant glint in her eye was Martha Williams S.C. And a caption running underneath that read:

"TYCOON ACCUSED OF LAUNDERING PROVO MILLIONS."

CHAPTER 8

in the always strange new
land of home

There was a place where Bill always went when he wanted to escape the troubles of his life. It was deep in the heart of the Wicklow mountains where the Avonmore river ran down from the black lake of Lough Tay into the brown lake of Lough Dan. It was a secret place in the old medieval oak forest unknown to most but the locals and it was to there that he repaired a few days after the ordeal of the Tribunal and the feeding frenzy of the media the morning after.

He lay low in his mansion for the first few days and let his office deal with the constant calls from reporters, bankers, friends, and business associates. He called his daughter in London. Mercifully she'd heard nothing of the sensational reports in the Irish papers. He reassured her it wasn't true, just some people jealous of his success out to get him. He knew his daughter would stand by him whatever wind would blow. His son in Clongowes would have heard something, but his life was so full of activity that it would wash over him and be gone like a bad nightmare. His wife was in the south of France and inured to Bill's travails. It wouldn't affect her lifestyle nor would he bother her with the grubby details. His staff were experts at handling the constant inquiries a man in Bill Cassidy's position invariably received and the increased interest as a result of the Tribunal was nothing they couldn't handle. In fact both Judy and Madeleine relished the challenge. They batted every inquiry away with all the exuberance of cricketers sending boundaries through silly mid-off or baseballers hitting home runs out of a stadium. Bill Cassidy brought out the predatory instinct in some females, the motherly instinct in others: lionesses protecting their lair. Having checked with them that the organization could withstand the siege and having received the relishing assurances that this was nothing they couldn't handle, he headed for the hills.

He threw some things in a bag because he'd probably go south after Wicklow. No point in languishing like a prisoner behind the security gates of his fortress-like residence feeling sorry for himself. The cleaning lady and the gardener would take care of things for a week or two. It was the Sunday after the time changed, less than a week left in March. The evenings would be longer and there was a change in the weather in the past few days. A gentle southwest wind was blowing and the delayed buds of spring were at last beginning to sprout. Daffodils

were blooming in long, serried lines on the sides and
centre meridian of the motorway as he headed past the
Sugarloaf and turned right before the Glen O'The
Downs. Up through Rocky Valley and onto the high
plateau of Callary Bog. He saw wide, green vistas
southward past Derrylossary and on towards Roundwood
and Annamoe. He was shaking the cloying grime of the
city from him like a butterfly shedding its cocoon. To the
right rose the rounded slopes of Djouce, farther back,
Kippure, and ahead, in the dim, blue distance,
Lugnaquilla and Glenmalure. He liked to let the names
roll off his tongue: Glendalough, Luggala, Avondale,
Glenmacnass. He turned right at the Roundwood Inn
and took the narrow back-road that headed down into
the deep, dark, luscious valley that he discovered over
twenty-five years before. Sometime after he came back
from California and started putting down roots in
Dublin. The time of his life which had intrigued Martha
Williams. Shrouded in foggy mystery like middle earth.

He parked where he always parked near the stone
bridge, built in 1828, that forded the rushing Avonmore,
and took the narrow trail down to the lake through the
great, branching trees. At last the birds were singing:
warbling thrushes, cawing rooks, tweeting goldfinches
and robins: all busy building nests. It had been a long,
cold, dreary winter. He walked on a carpet of shrivelled
oak leaves melting into the mossy track. There was a
rushing, rippling sound of running water as he crossed a
swollen stream that ran into the bigger river deep in the
woods. A stray dog took a liking to him and sniffed and
urinated its way along the trail in front of him like a

scout running ahead of advancing troops. How these
great oaks filled him with peace and delight. Some of
them may have been here nine hundred years: before the
battle of Kinsale, before Shakespeare wrote Macbeth,
some nearly saplings when Brian Boru fought the Danes
at Clontarf: *Cluain Tarbh*, the meadow of the bull. The
holly too was greening and the spreading willows, hazel
and alder near the water were showing tiny white and
green buds, like faint stars that first appear in the
evening sky. It was here that he first met up with Wild
Frank Russell on the set of some old tale of romance and
war and treachery that was being filmed in these
mountains and valleys by a Hollywood crew. Long before
the whips and scorns of time had made him cynical;
when life was still full of endless possibilities and the
road went on forever. Before Wild Frank had gone to the
happy hunting grounds and was still full of mirth and
guile and vigour and irreverence.

It was there by the lake twenty-five years ago that
they pitched their tents and bivouacked under the stars;
and killed Sir Uryens. Fierce blows rained down on his
armour-covered body as he was caught in a savage mêlée
by the mounted knights of the boy Mordred. He finally
succumbed by the sheer water's side to the clinging mud
and the cold rain.

Bill walked down to the lake, and no man-made
sound impinged upon his ears. Only birdsong, the dog
barking, the light wind sighing along the darksome lake.

But a darker image kept asserting itself: a white horse
dying under the blasted oaks with three cadavers hanging
high on the bare branches. That was a sad, strange day,

the day the white horse died; when the leaves were
coming on the oak trees in Childers Wood. Big-boned
and well made, it had carried him through many battles
against the dark Knights of the Round Table. In one
savage clash too many it strained its back in a muddy
swamp and couldn't extricate itself. They were in a
clearing under the trees and the horse suddenly lost its
action. Bill jumped off its back and the horse began to
shiver. It shifted its weight from one leg to the other. It
seemed to be getting worse. The morning was becoming
chilly. Bill looked at the sky and the trees. He looked at
the faces of the other knights; Wild Frank's face. He felt
dazed. The distant calls of the first unit crew could be
heard. The occasional cloud of smoke drifted by from
their incendiary devices. The girl groom got a bucket of
water and washed the white horse's hooves. It shifted its
weight from front to hind legs and then something
seemed to snap in its back. Suddenly it began to plunge
around, its legs dragging loosely behind it. It did not
whinny or neigh, or give any acknowledgement of the
pain that wracked its body. With one final desperate
effort it wheeled again, terror in its eyes, then crashed to
the shuddering earth. The trees seemed to creak and
bend in sympathy. The wind blew up, the morning grew
colder. The brave animal struggled to rise again but could
not rise itself. Its tail was limp. The young girl gently
cradled the white horse's head and uttered soothing
words. She placed a rug over its cold flanks. The vet
came at last. He stuck pins here and there in the dying
animal to test its reactions. There were none. The white
horse had no feeling left in its back. It was cracked for all

time. The vet took a pistol from a pouch. They all held
their breaths in dread. They hoped he wouldn't pull the
trigger but he did. There was a loud blast and the white
horse rose two feet off the ground, convulsed and then
fell back dead. To finish it off the vet drove a wire
through its forehead. The brains spilled out on the grass
like mustard. Bill felt sick. They took the white horse
away in a horsebox and the trees looked on impassively.
Slowly the morning sky cleared. By afternoon the sun
shone and almost all had already forgotten. But not
completely and not all. Bill would remember for many
years to come.

He walked back towards his car and wondered why this
image was so vivid today? He came here often and
usually never remembered. Was this a portent? He got
into his car and headed towards Glendalough. He drove
on past Laragh and followed the river to the meeting of
the waters in the Vale of Avoca. He headed south
through Gorey, historic Ferns, Enniscorthy and Vinegar
Hill. He turned west over the pleasant Slaney and
onwards past Clonroche to New Ross. Brooding
thoughts beset his journey. By afternoon he had crossed
the Suir in Waterford and headed west along the coast
past Wild Frank's grave. He stopped to see the rolling
waves on wide Clonea strand. He drove through
Dungarvan, crossed the Blackwater at Youghal and the
rich, fertile farmlands of east Cork flashed by. The
further on he went the less beset by troubles he became.
He took the Killarney road out from Cork City into the
dreamscape land of home. At Crookstown he branched

off on the Bantry Line through Béal na mBláth where Michael Collins died. It was dusk. On past Coppeen he went and the ambush site of the Battle of Kilmichael. History crowding in on every side. It was dark going through the Sheha mountains heading for Coosán Gap.

He saw a bright light in the sky to the south, too low to be a plane. It seemed to come from high in the hills off to the left. On a whim he swung off the main road and plunged down narrow, winding side roads. The climb went upward. He met nobody for a long time. He was somewhere south of Sheha and north of Owen. The closer he got to the light the more convinced he became that it was a fire. It would disappear out of sight behind huge rocks or clumps of trees and bushes, then re-emerge closer and brighter. He could now see the smoke and the outline of a building. He put his foot on the accelerator and the Jaguar surged forward, scratching and scraping off the briars and bushes on the narrow road. It spiralled upward and he guessed he was pretty high on the mountainside. There was a breeze fanning the flames. Now he could see ashes and sparks. He pulled out his mobile and called 999 frantically. He was maybe half a mile away. Ever higher. He got through finally to the operator. The reception was bad and breaking up. He managed to get the message across. Where the hell was he? He saw two men on the narrow road ahead of him running towards the fire. He slowed to a stop. They jumped in: Andy Blair and Peter McGregor of the new-age commune.

'Where are we, what's the name of this place, I'm on the phone to the fire brigade?'

'Cillaherlehane,'

'Cillaherlehane,' Bill shouted into the phone. 'Where's it near?'

'Three miles west of Coolkelure on the Bantry road, north of Castledonovan.' Bill relayed the information to the operator which the passengers just gave him. They swept into a farmyard. The house was a blazing inferno before their eyes. It was a thatched house.

'My God,' whispered Bill. They paused, momentarily paralysed. A burning house in the dark of night was an elemental thing. It instilled primal fear. Bill turned off the engine and jumped out. The other two jumped out with him. There was a roaring, crackling, ripping sound of flames. A sweetish smell of burning reed mingled with the acrid smell of burning felt. The heat hit Bill full in the face, there was a sour taste of smoke in his mouth. He heard the others shouting: 'George, George?'

They were running towards the old slate farmhouse across the yard.

'Who lives here?' he shouted.

'Over here,' replied Blair, 'he lives in this house.'

'Who's *he*?'

'George,' shouted Blair back. 'Want to make sure he's home.'

'What about the thatch?' shouted Bill.

'There's nobody living there yet,' shouted McGregor.

'Are you sure?' shouted Bill.

'Pretty much.' said the other.

Bill started forward. Which way to go? He looked up towards the flaming cottage. Instinct told him to go in that direction. The ridge-yealm was caving in; spraggers,

hazel liggers bent and shrivelled. Flames and sparks were
shooting high into the black sky, obscuring stars, half-
moon. There was more confused shouting. Blair and
McGregor, were trying to get a hose unravelled near the
old slate farmhouse. They had opened the door and
switched on a light. Bill made for the half-door of the
cottage. He got nearly as far as it but the heat drove him
back. He ran to the car and pulled out an old anorak and
threw it on, zipping it high to his chin and dragging the
hood over his head. He grabbed two gloves and charged
again for the door and burst it in with a shoulder charge.
The high vaulted ceiling was invisible; choking fumes
filled his lungs; overhead the whooshing roar of flames
devouring the rafters was deafening. He advanced to the
foot of the stairs, gasping for air. He could see a great
soaring chimney blackened and scorched. He would
have no more than a minute before his lungs burst.
'Hello, hello,' he shouted, 'anyone here?'

He pushed open a door leading to a downstairs
bedroom. Nobody in there. He'd have to retreat.
Couldn't climb that stairs. Then, just as he was
beginning to back away for the half door he saw the
outline of two boots, then the form of a man lying half
down the stairs. He grabbed the feet and pulled. The
man was heavy, and unconscious. He inched him
backward, foot by foot his lungs bursting, skin roasting.
Christ, this man was heavy. He stopped. Would he go
back for the others? He'd never get in again. He made a
superhuman effort. Then he was at the door and was
falling backward, his grip on the man faltering.

'Over here, over here,' he shouted. Then he seemed

to faint in a blackout with one foot outside the door and the man's head out but his feet still inside. He heard vague shouts and then the feel of arms pulling him out into the air to safety. He felt himself being pulled into the yard and slowly the rush of fresh air revived him. Then Blair and McGregor ran back and pulled the other man clear. Bill lay on the cobbled stone yard and looked up at the swirling smoke rising into the red and black sky. He rolled slowly over and pulled himself up and knelt on one knee, gasping. Eventually he said: 'Is he alright?'

'He's breathing,' said Blair, pumping at the man's chest beside him, prone on the cobbles. The yard was now full of people running in all directions and shouting loudly. The sound of the fire brigade siren reached their ears and two engines roared at high speed into the yard and ground to a halt. Shouting firemen ran around pulling hoses. The Fire Chief and two medics ran over to them. 'Anyone else inside d'you think?' he asked.

'Can't be certain,' said Blair.

'Who got him out?'

'That man there,' said Blair, pointing to Bill who was still down on one knee. The Fire Chief squatted down beside Bill.

'Did you see anyone else in there?' he asked.

'No,' said Bill, 'but it's hard to see anything with the smoke.'

'Does he have a family?' asked the Fire Chief.

'No, he lives alone,' said Blair.

In a matter of seconds huge jets of water were cascading over the burning building: the beautiful,

elaborately-woven ridge, the falling eave wadds, the
long and carefully laid stelches of blackened, burnt reed.
The people stood around shaking their heads as the
firemen worked frantically. It appeared to be too late.
The work of art was a desecrated ruin. The two medics
from the ambulance crew attended to the young man.
They were holding him, sitting up, putting water on his
face to cool him, getting him to drink.

'How are you sir?' the Fire Chief asked Bill.

'I'm okay,' said Bill, 'just a small blackout from lack
of oxygen. Look to the young man.'

'What's your name, sir?' asked the Fire Chief. Bill
told him.

'And the other young man?'

'No idea,' said Bill. 'Those other fellows know him. I
was driving west when I saw the flames. No idea who he
is. I just drove up to see what was happening.'

'Lucky for him you did,' said the Fire Chief. A
stretcher was produced from the ambulance and the
young man was slowly lifted onto it.

'How is he?' Bill asked the medic.

'He'll survive,' said the medic. 'Fume inhalation got
to him. Amazing he only has superficial burns; he'll pull
through; we'll take him to Bantry hospital straight away.
And yourself, do you want to come in the ambulance?'
Bill was now standing. He rubbed himself down, 'I think
I'm all in one piece,' he said, 'go ahead with him, I'll be
okay.'

'Maybe you'd want to check with the hospital just in
case,' said the Fire Chief.

'Thanks,' said Bill, 'I'm fine really. I'll check

tomorrow if I'm not feeling alright.' As the young man was being lifted into the ambulance, Andy Blair came over. Bill asked: 'Who is he do you know?'

'His name is George Conklin, he built the cottage,' said Blair. Bill turned slowly to him and thought he recognized him. 'Didn't we meet before?' he asked. Blair looked at him and then Peter McGregor came over and said: 'I think we met you in Keohane's bar in the town one night some months ago.' Bill looked from one to the other, then at the man being comforted in the ambulance.

'I remember,' he said, 'you're the Americans. I remember now. I was with Joey Harrison.'

The Fire Chief started writing down the names as the police arrived. Other neighbours crowded around. The firemen still worked on the flames which were slowly being doused, but the damage was already done. They were all silent. Then the Fire Chief said: 'It's a sorry sight.'

Sheridan, the sergeant came over and took their names all over again. The ambulance pulled out of the yard. The crowd milled around looking stunned. 'How did it happen?' somebody asked.

'Sure tis only just built,' said another, 'what could go wrong so soon?'

The Sergeant looked to the Fire Chief who had come back over from the other firemen. 'Any casualties?' asked the Sergeant.

'No,' said the Fire Chief, 'but twas a miracle this man happened to be passing below on the Bantry Line. He saw the flames.'

The Sergeant came over to Bill. 'I'm Sergeant
Sheridan,' he said.

'Pleased to meet you,' said Bill and shook his hand.
'Cassidy's the name. Bill Cassidy.' The Sergeant did a
double take: '*The* Bill Cassidy?' he asked.

'I'm afraid so,' said Bill.

'Glad to meet you,' said the Sergeant. 'You did a
mighty job by all accounts.'

'It's nothing.' said Bill. 'Listen I think I'll shove off if
you don't mind.'

'Where are you headed?' asked the Sergeant.

'I was going to Parknasilla for a few days, to the
hotel there.'

'That's a long drive,' said the Sergeant, 'are you sure
you want to go all that way tonight?'

'They're expecting me,' said Bill, 'I think I'll keep
going. I'll be fine'

'Would you mind if I called you in a day or two,' asked
the Sergeant, 'to take a bit of a statement about this?'

'No problem,' said Bill, 'I'd be glad to help. As long as
the young man is okay that's all that matters.' He gave
the Sergeant his number and slowly sat into his car and
started it up. The Sergeant said in parting: 'Don't let the
bastards grind you down.' Bill looked up at him quickly
but the Sergeant had already turned away. But Bill was
sure he'd heard correctly?

Some people shouted, 'Good luck, well done.' Bill
rolled down the car window. The crowd parted to let the
car through. The last words he heard from someone as
he drove out were: 'Twas the way some bad bastard burnt
it down.'

Bill drove out in the dark and suddenly realized he hadn't the faintest notion where he was. He looked at his watch. It was midnight. His head was swimming in a kind of dizziness that came in waves. He knew he was somewhere near Owen mountain but it was easy to get lost up here with the half moon obscured by cloud. You'd think you were going one way when it could be the opposite. Again he bemoaned the lack of satellite navigation the garage had urged upon him. He'd have to fall back on his boyhood nose for directions. He knew by the way the land was falling that he was probably heading south. The road twisted down past old, stunted birch trees. He'd never make Kenmare at this rate. Better stop closer to home. Maybe call on Joey? The last time things hadn't gone too well but each meeting with his old friend was a new beginning. Where their relationship stood was hard to tell. But it was deep, subterranean, full of old familiarities, fractiousness, the pleasure of common bonds, interests, acquaintances. The memories of old adventures long ago. Joey had no phone naturally so he couldn't ring in advance. But he was usually home in the early hours of the morning. It was worth a try.

He was now nearing somewhere familiar. He saw the lights of a village or small town down below. Off to the left was a stark and ghostly outline of a white cross on a far, distant hill. One of those Marian crosses put up in 1952, that always startled American or German tourists just as they thought they had a handle on the Irish. Not a bit of it. What was so different about the worship of the Virgin Mary on a cold mountain in the deep

southwest to the worship of the sun on Croagh Patrick
or Ben Bulben on the wild northern coast? This was still
a deeply spiritual and pagan land that believed in and
wished for magic, the rapture of the mystical, the
transports of necromancy. For the Americans and
Germans, with their traditions of pragmatism and
rationalism, mystery was hard to fathom. Which is why
they loved the whimsy of Ireland.

Drimoleague, that's where he was. Coming at it from
the north; the unfamiliar side. He joined the main road
on the western outskirts of the village and took the
signpost for Skibbereen. He was on home ground again.
Soon the lights of the town hove in sight. He drove
down North Street, quite deserted at this hour of night.
He passed the town hall and the post office on the left
and then followed the one-way system down Market
Street, back around by Drinagh Co-Op and Barry's
Builder's Providers until he was passing Thornhill's
Electrical from Townsend Street into Bridge Street and
looping back out the Ballydehob Road. He drove about
three miles with the Ilen river widening on his left. The
tide appeared to be out as he could vaguely discern the
great, grassy banks in midstream that were exposed at
low water and covered up when the full tide was setting
up from Baltimore. He turned left about three miles out
and went down a narrow boreen that led to Joey's house.
Just as he reached it the clouds cleared and there it rose
in front of him, brooding and mysterious, silhouetted
against the sky and the wide river bend. He turned off
the engine and got out. His lights had disturbed some
seabirds who squawked and flew. Otherwise there was no

sound, just the clinking of his engine cooling. He walked
towards the house and knocked on the moonlit door.
Silence. He knocked again. Nobody answered, only the
phantom listeners in the graveyard. He pushed the door.
Open as usual as was Joey's style. He tiptoed in slowly
and called Joey's name. Nobody home. He turned on a
side lamp and the chaos of the great kitchen greeted his
gaze. Empty wine bottles, the sink full of dirty dishes,
papers and half-opened books strewn on the scratched
oak table; the ancient record player still on with a .33
disc thumping round and round. He pressed the off
button and the record ran to standstill. He looked at the
title: Verdi's *Pezzi Sacre* conducted by Myung-When
Chung. Never heard of him, Chinese was he? The
soloist was Carmelia Remigio, soprano. Joey loved the
great sacred pieces: *Stabat Mater, Te Deum, Ave Maria.*
Bill felt he was intruding in spite of his long friendship
with Joey. There are parts of a man's soul you never got
to no matter how familiar. In fact the most obvious
secrets can be hidden in plain sight. Just as he turned to
walk out his eye caught a scrawled note that had fallen
to the floor. He picked it up. It read:

*"Rita, gone to Kinsale for a few days. There's coal in the
shed. Back in a few days."*

He hadn't signed it but Bill recognized Joey's
unmistakable scribble. He put the note back on the table
and went out. He started up the car and wondered where
to now? It was nearly two in the morning. The
Parknasilla Hotel in Kenmare was a good two hours

away. Besides, he was thinking about that young man he'd rescued from the fire. He'd stay in town and maybe visit the hospital in Bantry tomorrow. He drove back to Skibbereen and pulled in at the Eldon Hotel. He knocked. A sleepy concierge opened eventually. 'Can I help you?' he asked rather grumpily, looking Bill up and down. 'Sorry to call so late,' said Bill, 'but would you have a bed for the night by any chance?' The man hesitated and scrutinized Bill's dishevelled appearance again. Then some spark of recognition caused him to relent. 'Come in,' he said. He showed Bill to a nice room overlooking the street and went out. Bill looked at himself in the bathroom mirror and got quite a shock. His face was black and grimy, his hair in tangled knots, his shirt filthy and his tie askew. No wonder the man hesitated. Bill threw cold water on his face and dried it with some toilet paper. Then he threw himself on the bed and fell into a deep, dreamless sleep. In the always strange new land of home he was safe within his mother's valence, long forgotten but always there.

CHAPTER 9

a shaft of bright sunlight

Joey Harrison liked Kinsale: the romantic, winding streets, the Spanish and Elizabethan influences on the quaint buildings; the gourmet restaurants dripping with character and a sense of history: The Spaniard, Man Friday, The Bulman. He liked to wander out to the massive Charlesfort and look across towards the town and the harbour, and imagine Don Juan Del Aquila sailing in, in the year 1601 to send the English invaders back into the sea. What a balls-up that was. O'Neill and O'Donnell marching south:

> "O'er many a river bridged with ice
> And many a vale with snowdrifts dumb."

Surrounding the armies of Mountjoy and Carew in the hills behind the town; the Spanish between them and the ocean. It should have been a shoo-in. But no.

Murphy's law again. If something could go wrong it
would, with the Paddys at the wheel. As it was, the
whole business became a farcical rout. The Irish got
complacent or drunk or both, the Spanish funked it or
fucked it up as usual, and before you could say, *Lámh
Dearg Abú*, the game was over. Only for that fiasco we'd
all be speaking Irish around here, the Gaels would have
regained control of old Ireland, with the Brits
vanquished and European history looking completely
different. As it was, Mountjoy and Carew got their tails
up, sent the Northerners scampering home in disarray
and then proceeded with systematic plantation and
ethnic cleansing, (before the phrase was invented) to
drive the Celts to hell or to Connaught, grabbing the
best land for themselves and holding onto it for the next
four hundred years. Oh, some people would quibble over
details here and there but that was the gist of it more or
less in a nutshell. Give or take a score or fifty years one
way or t'other.

Come to think of it maybe he himself wouldn't be
here at all if the Brits lost. The Harrisons were bag-
carriers for Mountjoy and Carew, and probably hod-
carriers as well. When those two gallant boys burned and
slaughtered their merry way westward they parcelled out
a nice few hundred acres to the Harrisons on the banks
of the Ilen river as reward for their energetic cutting of
Gaelic throats in considerable numbers. But that was
neither today nor yesterday. Gradually the Harrisons
learned to drink poteen, married in to some local Irish
stock such as the McCarthys and O'Mahonys and
eventually emerged as blazing Republicans from 1798

onwards, red in tooth and claw; more Irish than the Irish themselves. Nothing soft about the Harrisons, which- ever way you took them.

But times changed. Faster in the last twenty years than in the previous four hundred. The Gaels were back on top: league leaders, Gold Cup winners, Triple Crown holders. And lashing money down to beat the band. Right now, Joey was sitting in the *uber* luxury of the visitors lounge of Bill Cassidy's flagship hotel, The Jamesfort. Red floral carpet three inches thick stretching as far as the eye could see; glittering Waterford chandeliers bigger than the moons of Jupiter twinkling away row on row into the dark, inviting ovum of the enormous building. Everything finished in mahogany and gold, like Trump Tower transferred to County Cork. The hotel stood on a hill above the town like a modern- day Charlesfort with panoramic views out along the coast to the Old Head to the west and Oysterhaven to the east. Northward you could see as far as the Galtee mountains and west to McGillicuddy's Reeks. Bill Cassidy certainly didn't do things by halves. Good luck to him.

Unbeknownst to Bill, Joey had been enjoying his hospitality for the past three days courtesy of *The Chronicle*. Tim Durkin had sent him down to snoop around after the sensational headlines in *The Irish Times* and that's what Joey was doing. Did Durkin think Joey was going to put a stiletto in his old friend's back? What did he think Joey Harrison was? Some kind of informer or fifth columnist? Worse still, did he take him for a fool? Well, Durkin had another think coming. Joey would recline here in the lap of luxury for as long as he possibly could, living high on the hog. Drinking the best Champagne, eating oysters on the half-shell with Guinness, gorging nightly on juicy sirloin and coiffing back bottles of Chateau Margaux 1975. Then in the fullness of time he'd come back with some cock and bull story that would tell Durkin exactly nothing that he didn't already know. Besides, Joey didn't buy that line from the Tribunal. Bill Cassidy involved with the Provos? Joey had known Bill a long time, over forty years. It didn't seem like his style. Sure, Bill, like many a self-made multi-millionaire in modern Ireland bought everybody he could and paid for everything that was buyable. That was the way capitalism worked and Joey had no time for it. But laundering paramilitary money was not Bill's style. He was too big and too shrewd for that. The Tribunal had underestimated him or else somebody was trying to set him up for a fall. Besides, Joey knew most of the big Provos over the years and he'd never heard so much as a whisper from them of the name Bill Cassidy. Joey smelt a rat and the longer he hung around the more convinced he was that the rat was somewhere nearby. Who'd have the motive to malign Bill? Somebody with everything to gain if he should stumble. Somebody who was close to him and had an understanding of how his business worked and the extent of his assets. Who knew how valuable those assets were.

In the last few days Joey had struck up a friendship with a girl named Corinne Daly, one of the public relations people employed by the hotel. She went around meeting people and greeting new guests, especially those who stayed longer than a night or two and who appeared to spend money in the bar and restaurants. With his healthy expense account Joey soon became a target for Corinne's attention. Besides he'd made a special effort to smarten up his image. He'd dusted down the old Harris tweed suit that was mothballed in the house for years and he'd polished up his best Salamander brogues and made sure to sport a cravat or spotted hankie in his top pocket. But the jewel was the car. He had a vintage Mercedes locked in the shed for the past twenty-five years and he decided to give it a run to Kinsale for the occasion. It was in perfect working order, one of the few things in his life that was: shining and smelling of the best leather. When Corinne saw Joey coming and going in that she assumed he was a gentleman of substance and certainly the first part of that description was accurate, whatever about the substance part. He told her he was a solicitor which was true, but the fact that he didn't practise was neither here nor there. She soon started to sit down beside him more than a few times in the past couple of days. He could see she was becoming fascinated by his impeccable manners with women and his sparkling, witty conversation. Joey could be quite the lady's man when it suited him. And women always sensed that he liked them. In fact Joey placed women on a pedestal and had done so all his life, starting with his mother. And of course Joey was a sucker for her type. She was tall and thin and had movie star looks, aged twenty-five or six. She kept her hair tied back in a pony tail and beneath the highlighted blonde one could see darker roots at the base. What a turn on. Her eyes were deep brown and set wide apart giving her a kind of Slavic look although she was definitely Irish, pure south county Dublin. Probably a Mount Anville girl who knew just the right buttons to push with older men and so aware of her attractiveness that it gave her a lot of power. Some days she came in with a slight puffiness under her eyes, her full mouth slightly bruised-looking and her voice a hoarse, husky whisper. What had she been up to last night? Those slight flaws on her otherwise flawless, sallow skin had Joey Harrison throbbing with sexual tumescence. Mother of God, she would drive him mad with lust. By day four they'd become firm friends and Joey was daring to dream of further possibilities. Was he a damn, deluded fool? Men of his age were not as potent in the loins as they once had been. Joey hoped what he'd lost in the power of the shanks he'd make up for in finesse. Dream on.

He'd seen the other high-ups around here coming and going in the last few days, but he was anxious to keep a low profile. Didn't want anybody to tumble to the fact that he was a reporter. That fair-haired fellow floated around most days meeting and greeting. He'd nod at Joey but it appeared that Joey was Corinne's booty so he'd come no nearer. Corinne said his name was Laurence O'Grady, the assistant manager. Joey took long stock of him over a number of days: plausible, yes, smooth certainly, but was he smart enough to be *Judas Iscariot*? Unlikely. He looked too much of the rugger-bugger to have the brains for subterfuge.

The other *rara avis* less often sighted was the tall, sad-looking fellow with the inscrutable face whom Corinne said pulled the strings. Brian Bracken, by name. Joey would see him occasionally speaking low with O'Grady or Corinne outside the door inhaling deeply on a cigarette. He looked nervous, almost furtive. Now there, thought Joey, was a specimen who could merit a little more microscopic scrutiny. Joey started throwing curve balls around. He never asked Corinne directly about Bracken as he'd learnt long ago that one of the best rules of writing was: thou shalt not write on the nose. Never be too obvious. This dictum applied to most things in life. A bit of hither and over would be more effective: circle the prey, duck and dive, then when the opportunity presented itself, in for the kill. Corinne had already divulged that Bracken was a workaholic who never took holidays; he liked to control everything despite having a seemingly innocuous, low-key approach. He was rarely seen with women, but whereas Corinne knew that he fancied herself, in the way a woman's radar detects what a man is thinking from two miles away, he never hit on her directly. Wonder why, thought Joey? He was single, she was the obvious trophy around here for any upwardly mobile ambitious man. Was he homosexual? Didn't look it. No, he must have some other, hidden agenda. It didn't take Joey long to stumble across it.

There was a big influx of guests coming in for the weekend. Friday night saw the start of the Law Society of Ireland's annual conference. Corinne assumed Joey was part of it. He didn't tell her that he'd rather have his fingernails pulled out with pliers than spend the

weekend with that boring bunch of self-satisfied
dullards. But he suddenly saw it as an opportunity to
make a major breakthrough. He'd invite Corinne out to
dinner away from the madding crowd of babbling
lawyers, ply her with Dom Perignon and Pina Coladas
until she dropped her guard. Then he'd probe her until
she gave him the goods on Bracken and with a bit of
luck get a bit of probing of another variety in as well.
Kill two birds with one stone so to speak. This would be
a delicate operation.

'Look, Corinne,' he said to her casually in the middle
of the Friday afternoon as the first contingent of
solicitors arrived, 'why don't you and I slip away this
evening and have a bit of supper.'

Corinne smiled and repeated: 'A bit of supper?' She
was already charmed by the old-world phraseology that
Joey employed so deftly, 'I don't think I've ever had a bit
of supper before.'

'Well, dinner then if you want to employ common
American semiotics,' said Joey.

Corinne didn't need too much persuasion. The lobby
was beginning to fill up with stentorian voices and loud
laughs that bespoke vacant minds. Here came the rugby-
shirted, jean-clad, 'dube'-wearing yahoos, hell-bent on
partying till the cows came home. Both male and female
of the species liked to dispense with the pinstripes, the
collars and ties and the horsehair perukes when they
went out on the razz. Corinne took one look at the
invading hordes and said: 'What time is supper then?'

'Let's say eight bells?' suggested Joey, 'at Man Friday.'

'Sounds perfect,' she said huskily.

Man Friday was one of the more discreet and up-market gourmet restaurants in a town renowned for its Good Food Circle. It was tucked away off the beaten track across the harbour on the road over to Charlesfort in what they called the Scilly district. You were transported to a tropical Caribbean ambience from the moment you descended the flower-strewn steps under the overhead bamboo canopy and into a world of teak and cut glass and pictures on the walls that might have been painted by Gauguin. It was spread out on four levels including a conservatory with elevated views over the inner harbour. Palm tree stump seats surrounded the central bar. It was here the vacationing super-yacht owners or visiting businessmen came to unwind after a long, hard day on the golf course or the broad Atlantic. If ever somebody was going to 'fess up and let down their guard it was here and Joey was so excited at the prospect of what was to come he could hardly breathe. My God, if the girl only knew the rather squalid reality of his life. But did he not deserve a little romance, a little pleasure? Some *joie de vivre* before he shuffled off the mortal coil?

They were shown to a discreet table under a large picture depicting a line of cypress trees stretching into the lush distance. From this cosy corner they could observe the comings and goings of the great and good, yet remain anonymous themselves in the penumbrous shadows. Joey had a dry Sherry to get off the mark and Corinne a sweet Chardonnay. The menu was a conundrum, with a bewildering choice of mouth-watering offerings. For the entrée Joey eventually plumped for the crab *au gratin*, to be followed by the grilled escalopes of monkfish with roasted peppers, and sundried tomatoes with a light wine sauce. Corinne chose six oysters poached in their own juices in a delicate *beurre blanc* sauce, and duck *ardmadnac* with nectarine and brandy sauce for the main course. The place was filling up nicely and the buzz was palpable. Joey ordered up a bottle of Chateau De La Negly Coteaux Du Languedoc and they toasted their new friendship. To Joey it was obvious that the trump card for the older man in his relationship with a younger female was neither his money or his looks but in fact his knowledge and sophistication. Girls were suckers for that. That and a good sense of humour. For some reason that was nearly always top of the list. Always baffled him. You could be a *clochard* but if you made her laugh you were halfway there. Were women eternal romantics? Of course it helped if you were a good listener. Joey was definitely that.

They were well into the main course and he'd ordered the second bottle of the Chateau De La Negly. The mixture of the Grenache and the local grape was really so good it would chew the face off of ten Chateauneuf du Papes; a great whack of fruit with overtones of white pepper. Addictive. Joey filled both glasses and held his up to the light and tilted it a little. Then he broached the subject of Bill Cassidy.

'I haven't seen him around,' said Corinne, 'but that's not surprising. He only visits about once a month and then leaves the morning after.'

'He's probably keeping a low profile after all those newspaper headlines,' said Joey, 'I know I would.'

'I agree,' said Corinne, 'I'd be mortified.'

'But you know these businessmen, they've got necks like a jockey's bollocks, it just washes over them.'

Corinne convulsed in gales of laughter, 'I like your apt description,' she said and took another quaff of her drink. Joey took another draught as well and then paused before asking her: 'What's he like anyway, ever met him?'

'I've met him but I don't know him well. He mainly deals with Brian Bracken. I get the impression he's quite remote. As regards the staff anyway.'

'That's probably a self protective mechanism. I wouldn't blame him for being remote after what's happened to him lately.'

'Oh, definitely,' she said, 'but he never bothers me so I must be doing a good job.' She wrinkled her nose coyly. What a fox. How would he keeps his paws off her?

'So how does he keep in touch, if he's never there?' asked Joey casually.

'He gets a daily report on his computer, plus a weekly report and a monthly as well.'

'Really,' said Joey, 'so he's well on top of things?' Corinne didn't appear to suspect anything. Good. Things were getting quite cosy. He'd press on delicately: 'So what do you really think?'

'About what?'

'This whole Provie business and Bill Cassidy. Do you believe that?'

'God, I don't know.'

'My question is this, why would a guy as rich as Bill Cassidy bother to mess around with laundered paramilitary money? For what? He can make all the money he wants legitimately, don't you think?'

'You know…' she was about to say something and paused and took a quick look around at the other diners, 'better keep our voices down.'

'I agree,' said Joey, 'the walls have ears.' He decided to cool the jets.

'How do you like this red?' he asked, 'has a nice bouquet doesn't it?'

'I wouldn't know,' she said, 'that's all far too complicated for me. How do you learn about wine anyway?'

'Well there's only one surefire way and that's to start drinking it. Which I wouldn't recommend to a young lady like you, except in small doses.'

'Why, think I'd become addicted?'

'You have time enough to become addicted my dear, when you're an old fogey like me. But my advice would be to mind your liver for as long as you can.'

'Did you see that movie, *Sideways?*'

'One of my favourites,' said Joey, 'I rarely go to the cinema anymore but I loved that. Laughed my ass off.'

'So you like Pinot Noir?'

'As a matter of fact I do. I like a lot of the New World wines. The problem with Pinot Noir is you can't get a decent bottle for less than fifty Euros. Otherwise it's just rubbish.'

'Really, well I won't be drinking much of that then.' She paused and looked slowly around again, and then lowered her voice: 'You know, to get back to the Bill Cassidy business, something has been bothering me for a bit but I never told anyone.'

'What do you mean?' asked Joey, leaning forward.

'About what we were discussing, the money laundering and all that?'

'Yeah?'

'Quite frankly it stinks,' she blurted out.

'What does?' asked Joey, feigning puzzlement. She faltered again and looked around her: 'I shouldn't say this...' she stopped again, searching Joey's face and leaning in close across the table.

'I'm afraid you have me there,' said Joey. Corinne continued to look deep into his eyes as if testing him.

'Oh, what the heck,' she said finally, 'what do you care, you're not a party to any of this, so I'll tell you a theory.'

'I wish you would,' said Joey, 'the suspense is killing me.' She took a long draught from her glass and carefully replaced it and began running her finger around the rim as if she was nervous. Joey took a sip and regarded her steadily. She seemed to be struggling to find the words. At last she began: 'Brian Bracken is a very ambitious man. He's worked for Bill Cassidy for at least five years. During that time he's seen Bill going from strength to strength without putting his back out, with very little input in the day to day running of the operation. Bracken feels he's doing the donkey work and he's not being appreciated for it.'

'Or rewarded?' suggested Joey.

'Or rewarded,' repeated Corinne.

'But surely he must know Bill has more than one iron in the fire?'

'Of course he does. He knows Bill works on all sorts of different levels, but he feels this hotel is his own baby because he has nursed it into being. He's identified the customer base, he's driven up the numbers and devised the marketing strategy.'

'By employing such a trump card as yourself,' said Joey with a grin. She shrugged: 'Whatever about me, the one thing about my position is that I have gotten close to the workings of the administration of the place in the past year and a half.'

'So Bracken has let you into the inner sanctum?'

'Not quite, Bracken would never do that. He's very careful. For instance he never screws around with any of the staff although I know through the grapevine that he's quite the stud away from home.'

'Really,' exclaimed Joey, 'I figured there was something too wholesome about him to be true.'

'Oh, don't you worry, Brian is anything but wholesome. He's sneaky and ruthless and he feels he's more educated than Bill. He resents Bill's success despite the lack of letters after Bill's name. Brian has a business degree, a master's I think. He'd also love to boast that he owns The Jamesfort and be the big shot around here. And he's identified the one weakness Bill has.'

'What's that?'

'He delegates too easily, without double-checking on his staff.'

'You mean he's too trusting?'

'Exactly. Bill has a naivety about him that has made him very rich but could also be his undoing.'

'Well, for somebody who knew very little about Bill an hour ago, you're suddenly a mine of information,' laughed Joey.

'Must be the wine,' she said, 'it loosens the tongue.'
Joey made a face. She noticed: 'But not necessarily
anything else, so don't you be getting any ideas, Mister.'

'What?' smiled Joey, feigning innocence.

'I saw that lascivious look in your eyes, you old
devil. Don't try to fool me.'

'My dear young lady, you'd make a snowman
lascivious,' said Joey with his most charming grin.

'What am I going to do with you?' she replied,
flattered, and slapped the back of his hand.

'Don't worry about me, I'm old enough to be your
father.'

'The older the fiddle the sweeter the tune,' she said
provocatively.

'Mother of God,' said Joey, 'you'll give me a heart
attack.' He dragged the back of his hand across his
heated brow: 'Better get back to what you were saying
before I pole-vault out of here.'

Corinne doubled up with laughter. 'You really are
something,' she said and paused. Then she continued,
getting serious again: 'Anyway, there is one final thing I
was leading up to. Brian Bracken has been allowing me
a few insights into the way he works, quite by accident I
should add. You see he's such a chauvinist he thinks I'm
just a dumb blonde, whom he sends out to attract the
customers and little else. He also knows I'm good on
computers. One day he couldn't get into his personal
email, some virus or other, so he asked me could I sort it
out. He gave me his password and I solved his problem.
There were dozens of emails there that he hadn't
deleted, just boring routine stuff and I guess he figured I

wouldn't bother reading them or else I wouldn't be
interested; which I wasn't, except for a few. One was
from somebody in a Tribunal in Dublin to him and it
said something to the affect that they appreciated his
information, it was extremely helpful. I was curious
naturally and began looking back through older emails
until I came across one from Brian to a Martha Williams
and it said:

> *"I'm sure Mr. Cassidy isn't doing everything above board,
> but I can't exactly prove it yet, but I'm working on it."*

I kept looking until I found another exchange of emails.
The gist of them was asking Brian would he come to the
next meeting of the Tribunal and act as a witness against
Bill. His reply was that he'd be happy to, but he'd rather
not appear the first day as it would look too obvious.
Words to that effect. A last email asked him if he had
anything specifically that would incriminate Bill.
Bracken's reply was that he hadn't but he asked wouldn't
the adverse publicity nail him one way or the other. To
say someone was sympathetic with the IRA and possibly
laundering their money was surely very damaging. The
reply was that bad publicity itself was not tantamount to
a crime but certainly it could cause an erosion of public
confidence in Mr. Cassidy that eventually might reap
rewards.'

'You know,' said Joey, 'you've confirmed my
suspicions. I always felt there was something that didn't
sound right about Bill Cassidy dealing with the Provos.
And I think you've cracked it. This fellow Bracken is

trying to damage Cassidy by linking him to para-militaries by innuendo and gossip.'

'He has no proof of any of it.'

'No, nor will he have, because it isn't true. This is like a form of blackmail. It's pure defamation and Bracken is obviously hell bent on trying to destroy Bill Cassidy by hook or by crook.'

Joey took another sip of his drink and said: 'That's pretty explosive stuff if you read between the lines. The Tribunal lawyer is being careful not to commit herself directly but she certainly is aiding and abetting Bracken's fraud and libel, because that what it is. But can you prove the emails are there? You said you deleted them.'

'Only after I sent copies of them to my own laptop,' she said.

'What a clever girl,' said Joey admiringly, 'and there he was thinking you were just a pretty face.'

Corinne sat back with a self-satisfied smile like the cat with the cream when suddenly her face clouded and she put down her head. 'Don't look,' she said, 'but Brian Bracken has just walked in.'

'Where?' asked Joey

'Don't let him see you looking whatever you do. He's just come in with a woman. They're gone to a table out in the conservatory, I think.'

'Well, I bet his ears are burning,' said Joey, 'speak of the devil and he'll appear. Look, we're nearly finished anyway. We'll wait till they're seated and then sneak out.' Joey called for the tab and soon the waiter brought it down to them. Joey took out a credit card. Corinne glanced quickly at it. Joey wrote out the amount and left

an elaborate tip. Then they got up and slipped out past
the bar. Corinne went on ahead and Joey stole a look
towards the conservatory. He saw Bracken immediately
although his back was to him, but his height gave him
away. But who was the woman? Joey had seen her before.
He wracked his brains. His photographic memory was
letting him down. She looked the image of the movie
actress, Kristin Scott Thomas, but surely it wasn't her?
Not unless Bracken was getting into show business.
They got their coats and as they were standing waiting
for the porter to bring up Joey's old Mercedes he clicked
his fingers and said: 'It's her, the one from the Tribunal.'

'Who do you mean?' asked Corinne.

'The woman with Brian Bracken, it's Martha
Williams from the Tribunal.'

'Martha Williams are you sure?'

'Certain,' said Joey, 'I never forget a face. She was on
the paper the same day as Bill, the day of the front page
publicity from the Tribunal.'

'You really think so?'

'I said to myself the day I saw her picture, I took a
special note of it, I said to myself, there's that actress,
then I realized she was the Counsel for the Tribunal, no,
there's no doubt. And after what you told me it makes all
the sense in the world.'

'But why would she come down here so obviously?'
asked Corinne.

'That Law Society Conference, she'd have come with
a bunch of legal types, the perfect cover. And I can see
now what you meant about Bracken never screwing on
his own patch. He doesn't need to. He's got her.'

'Do you think they're...you know...having it off together?' asked Corinne.

'What do you think?' asked Joey, 'Kinsale, the weekend, the Man Friday, a half moon in the April sky, a nightingale singing in Berkeley Square.'

'Killing two birds with one stone,' said Corinne, nodding.

'Speaking of which?' said Joey and gave her his most smouldering look. 'You old devil,' she said and leant over and suddenly kissed him. Joey thought he'd faint standing up in his shoes.

They drove slowly back to the hotel. Joey was apprehensive but entirely resigned to his usual fate of a peck on the cheek and a firm handshake. But the wheel of fortune can sometimes take a strange turn. Balanced on the cusp of acceptance or rejection he was modest in his expectations. But the Gods were smiling on him and like a shaft of bright sunlight that breaks through the clouds on a gloomy day and illuminates an object for an instant, the light shone on Joey.

He passed a night of unexpected and unheralded bliss. His tired old wildest dreams were suddenly realized in the arms of this nubile and most beautiful girl. Oh, Joey, what had he done to deserve this? Old memories, old pains were buried and forgotten once and for all time. She gave him her favours without holding back and Joey Harrison was for one beautiful moment, eager and reborn, and all life's petty disappointments, humiliations and defeats were put to flight. Old ghosts and gremlins danced in the moonlight and gave proof through the night that love was all there was and made the world go round. If only for a night, but one night was sufficient.

When he awoke next morning the bed was empty, but her fragrance still lingered on the sheets and he brought a white handkerchief along with him that she had left behind to remind himself that there was still life left in the old dog and he wasn't ready for the boneyard yet. He left a dozen red carnations for her at the reception desk and drove west with the rising sun behind him onto the roads of grace.

CHAPTER 10

the roads of grace

He heard the news on the car radio coming into Clonakilty. He was humming *Bonnie Annie Lawrie* to himself, that magnificent traditional Scottish ballad:

"'But for bonnie Annie Lawrie
I'd lay me down and dee.'"

Playing on Lyric FM. Wonder who the tenor was? A Russian, he thought he heard the announcer say. And the beautiful window boxes in bloom on every sill: marsh marigolds, geraniums, heathers; Clonakilty was gone very chic. Damn, the song was ended with no credits. Then the sucker punch: the first item on the 11 o'clock news: a thatched cottage destroyed by fire late last night in the hills above Drimoleague near Owen mountain; a man severely injured and detained in

Bantry hospital suffering the affects of third degree burns
and smoke inhalation. The fire brigade units from
Dunmanway, Skibbereen and Bantry had responded to
an emergency call from a passing motorist and had
rushed to quell the blaze. The motorist had single-
handedly rescued the injured man from the burning
building, which was completely gutted. Fortunately
nobody else was hurt. The cottage had only recently
been completed by a young American man new to the
locality.

Joey continued to listen in a kind of stupor as the
broadcast mentioned some other details about the
location and the owner, whose name was George
Conklin, originally from California. The Fire Chief and
the local police under Sergeant Sheridan were fulsome
in their praise of the rescuer whose name was Bill
Cassidy, the well known entrepreneur who hailed
originally from West Cork.

Bill Cassidy? Had he heard correctly? What was Bill
Cassidy doing on Owen mountain at midnight? There
must be some mistake. Joey pulled the car in onto the
footpath and nearly knocked a pedestrian down in his
haste. He ignored the double yellow line as he dashed
into Meade's newsagents and grabbed *The Irish Examiner*.
His eyes devoured the front page. There it was at the
bottom:

"WELL KNOWN BUSINESSMAN IN DRAMATIC FIRE RESCUE."

The article went on to repeat almost verbatim the gist of

the radio announcement a few minutes earlier. He paid for the newspaper and returned to his car and drove slowly out of town. The morning was bright and sunny, then suddenly the sky darkened in a sudden squall, then brightened again. The weather seemed to reflect his thought patterns. One moment lost in the ecstasy of last night, the next moment a deep frown furrowing his brow as if he didn't quite trust what his eyes and ears were telling him about Bill Cassidy rescuing the American George Conklin from the blazing thatch. What kind of coincidence was that? How could he have come across the fire? It wasn't supposed to happen like this. The American seriously injured in hospital. What if he died? Christ, Joey was beginning to sweat.

As he passed Rosscarbery the sun came back out again and shone down like honey on scores of white swans floating like stately galleons on the blue-green waters on either side of the causeway bisecting the estuary. It was one of those early spring days with winter still dragging at its heels and yellow buttercups, snowdrops and daffodils dancing in the breeze. On the narrower stretches of the road west of Leap and Union Hall sudden pure-white splashes of blackthorn buds heralded the full bloom of spring not far away. In orchards, apple and plum trees were showing their first snowy blossoms; crows' nests appeared on the high, bare branches of ash, sycamore and beech trees, while the cawing, fractious rooks flew from branch to branch and pecked and harried their bumptious way across grassy fields in search of twigs and other debris to complete their annual imperative to hatch their fledglings. In the face of nature's bustle Joey wracked his brains and tried to formulate some kind of coherent plan in anticipation of the coming fury.

Bill Cassidy woke with a headache and a body sore in every joint. He sat up in bed and slowly took stock of his surroundings. Where was he? Yes of course, the Eldon Hotel in Skibbereen. And hadn't he rescued a young man from a burning house in the middle of the previous night? Was it true or did he dream it? He gingerly got out of bed and felt his aching limbs: arms, elbows, shoulders, back. The effort of hauling the man to safety was obviously greater than he realized. One had superhuman strength on such occasions, fuelled by excitement and adrenalin. He was in no doubt once he saw his blackened shirt and bedraggled clothes. He'd have to get those cleaned. He would dress himself slowly in a clean shirt, jacket and trousers from the suitcase that he didn't even remember bringing in last night. But first he shaved and showered and by the time he'd dressed he was feeling considerably better. He made his way downstairs into the breakfast room. The waitress greeted him with a friendly smile and he ordered orange juice, toast and coffee. He picked up the local morning paper and the first name he saw on the front page was his own, standing out in bold italics. A laudatory article recounting his exploits of the previous night sung his praises and applauded his courage. He'd gone from villain to hero in the space of one short week.

He finished his breakfast and paid at the front desk. Would Mr. Cassidy be staying another night? Perhaps, he'd let them know later. He'd leave his car in the car park if that was alright? Absolutely Mr. Cassidy, anything you want. Bill took a stroll downtown. You'd hardly call it a town, more an *up the main street down the same street* kind of place; but he felt quite at home here although not exactly a townie. He saw many familiar faces. He noticed people looking after him as he was passing the old Mart car park, the Wine Vaults bar and on down to Hickeys newspaper shop. He bought *The Irish Times* and there on the second page was his name again. Wonder what those Tribunal people would say now? If he knew them probably nothing. They liked to ignore anything that didn't serve themselves. God forbid somebody should appear as a human being and do some good. Once you were a target you could do nothing positive in their eyes. All your life's achievements counted for naught. Thankfully the public didn't think like that. Public opinion changed quickly because the public saw both sides of the story.

He turned into Keohane's bar and sat down at one of the nice pine tables. The bar looked more inviting in the daytime. Almost atmospheric. There was a smell of fresh coffee, and freshly baked bread. People were having elevenses and he saw some more people he knew. He could relax here. He was dressed casually in an open-necked shirt, jacket and slacks. He felt pretty good despite his exertions of the night before. Michael Murphy and Tim Durkin were walking out. He knew Murphy from one or two real estate transactions. Murphy came over all smiles: 'Hello, Bill, my word you're getting yourselves in the paper a lot these days.'

'Hello, Michael,' said Bill and didn't stand. But shook his hand.

'You know Tim Durkin,' said Murphy, 'Editor of *The Chronicle.*'

'Pleased to meet you, Tim,' said Bill, 'I don't believe I've had the pleasure.'

'My goodness, that was some feat of bravery on your part last night,' said Murphy, 'I'm surprised you're up and about so early.'

'It was just a stroke of good fortune I was passing,' said Bill. 'I did what anybody would do in the circumstances. No big deal in the end.'

'You're being too modest old chap,' said Murphy, 'the story is you saved this man single-handedly and he unconscious in the blazing house.'

'That's not quite true,' said Bill, 'there were two other fellows who helped in the end. They were very courageous.'

'Oh, I think you're trying to give them too much credit,' said Durkin, 'our reporter says you were the hero of the hour.'

'Well, it's nice to be called that for a change,' said Bill. An awkward silence followed. These two men of the world would have been well aware of the Tribunal reports on Bill, but nobody wanted to mention the war. No doubt when they left they would have a hearty old gossip about him but people like Bill always fascinated and commanded respect. They both knew that in the scheme of things he was a far bigger fish than either of themselves.

'Are you all alone?' asked Murphy.

'As a matter of fact I am,' said Bill, 'I was actually

going to Parknasilla for a few days to kick back when this all happened.'

'There's never a dull moment with a man like you,' said Durkin with grudging admiration, 'I'm surprised your entourage isn't here to support you.'

'Entourage,' laughed Bill, 'believe it or not I eat by myself most nights, despite what people might imagine.'

'Oh, now, don't expect us to believe that,' said Durkin. 'I was talking to a good friend of yours only the other day. Singing your praises he was.'

'Really, who's that?' said Bill.

'Joey Harrison,'

'Joey Harrison,' laughed Bill, 'singing my praises. That'll be the day.'

'But he's a great admirer of yours,' said Durkin.

'I'll believe that when I hear it from the horse's mouth,' said Bill. 'By the way where is he? I went to his house late last night and there was nobody home.'

'You never know with Joey.' said Durkin, 'he could be anywhere. Will o' the wisp and all that.'

'I would have thought the opposite,' said Bill evenly. 'I would have thought of Joey as a creature of very regular habits. At least in the old days when I knew him. And a man gets even more conservative as he gets older.'

'That's very true,' said Murphy and looked at his watch.

'Doesn't he work for your paper?' Bill asked Durkin.

'He writes a few articles for us,' said Durkin with a sudden, slight stammer.

'More than a few from what I hear,' said Bill, 'isn't he your star columnist?'

'Star is hardly the apposite word,' laughed Durkin nervously, his treble chins trembling, 'but he is colourful.'

'Colourful?' inquired Bill, 'I hear he's the reason people buy your paper every Saturday. To see what Joey Harrison is doing to save the neighbourhood and bring jobs to town.'

'He does have influence, but not quite as much as he'd like you to believe himself,' said Murphy. 'He's also quite controversial.'

'Well, I heard he's a bit of a one man band for raising awareness about the prospects for industry in this area.'

'He must have told you that himself,' smiled Murphy but the humour had left his eyes. 'There are a few more of us who also do our bit around here. Anyway Bill, I'm glad to see you're in good shape after your ordeal. Congratulations again.'

'Thanks Michael,' said Bill.

'It was nice meeting you at last,' said Durkin unctuously, 'we've been hearing so much about you. You are quite the legend you know.'

'A local hero, eh?' said Bill ironically.

'The best kind,' said Durkin.

They walked out and Bill sat looking after them. Why did Durkin stammer when talking about Joey? People often did that when talking about their business. Often with something to hide. Did he know Joey was in Kinsale as the note said? It would be interesting to find out. They both seemed uncomfortable talking about Joey come to think of it. Did they know more than they let on?

They had no sooner left when the proprietor, Jim Keohane walked in. He saw Bill and came hurrying over: 'Bill Cassidy, Bill Cassidy, the man of the moment,' he gushed effusively.

'Hello Jim,' said Bill, a little surprised at Keohane's enthusiasm. It went against the grain. Keohane was a poor actor. But what could he do? Bill was all over the papers; the hero of the hour. If it was the previous headline a guy like Keohane wouldn't be so keen. He was the kind who ran with the hare and hunted with the hounds. This time he had no choice. He sat down beside Bill and shook his head in phoney disbelief:

'My God, that was a miracle. How did you manage it?'

'Good fortune I guess,' said Bill.

'That young man's good fortune anyway.' said Keohane. 'You met him here first you know.'

'I believe I did,' said Bill.

'Damn right you did, the last time you were here, the night with Joey Harrison. Remember three fellas walked in, hippie types.'

'Yes I remember, I think I spoke to them.'

'That's right, you introduced yourself as you left.'

'It's a small world,' said Bill.

'Unbelievable,' said Keohane, 'unbelievable.'

'So, what's the story on it?' asked Bill, 'was it arson or what?'

'Hard to say,' said Keohane, 'a lot of people knew about that cottage. Twas a kind of curiosity around here. And you know with straw. It can catch fire easy.'

'Come on,' said Bill, 'the place was only just built. No one living in it. It had to be arson.'

Keohane looked around to ensure no one was listening and leant in towards Bill, lowering his voice:

'Well, of course there are rumours going around already.'

'About the culprit?' asked Bill.

'Exactly,' said Keohane, his voice now a confidential whisper.

'And who might that be?' asked Bill.

'Oh then, a man we both know reasonably well if I may say so,' and he winked knowingly.

'Well there's not too many who fit that category,' said Bill, 'so you must be talking about Joey Harrison.'

'Don't say I said it because I didn't,' said Keohane, 'but a lot of people are saying it.'

'And what motive would Joey have?' asked Bill.

'Sure didn't you hear him the last night yourself. Ranting against every foreigner coming into the country.'

'I've known Joey a long time,' said Bill. 'His bark is worse than his bite, especially when he gets drunk.'

'Ah, but we had blue murder here some months ago at a council meeting. He threatened all sorts of violence against a bunch of the environmental crowd opposing a new development. Thrown out of the meeting he was. There was war.'

'Really,' said Bill, 'but surely Joey is not alone in his opinions.'

'There are others of course,' said Keohane, 'but Joey is the one who does all the shouting.'

'But maybe that's all he does,' said Bill. Keohane nodded to himself and said no more. Then he stood up from the table and said: 'You'll have a drink?'

'A bit early for drinking,' said Bill.

'For the occasion that's in it,' said Keohane.

'Hardly an occasion to be celebrating,' said Bill.

'Not at all,' said Keohane, 'tisn't every day you save a man from a burning house. You'll have a whiskey.'

'Very well then,' said Bill. Keohane moved back inside the counter. Bill got up from the table and walked to the bar. He stood beside an older man with a kindly face sitting on a stool and said hello. 'You know Cornelius Canty?' said Keohane.

'Pleased to meet you, Cornelius,' said Bill and shook his hand.

'So,' said Bill to Keohane, 'do you have any more information on who this man is?'

'Not a whole lot,' said Keohane, 'but there's a man who knows him well.'

'Is that so?' said Bill.

'That man built the thatch with him, didn't you Cornelius.'

'A lot of good twas for me,' said Cornelius sadly. 'All our work in vain.'

'I'm mighty sorry to hear it,' said Bill, 'it must be very disheartening for you.'

'A terrible business,' said Cornelius, 'a terrible business altogether.'

'You must have put a lot of work into it,' said Bill.

'The world wide of it,' said Cornelius, 'twas a beautiful job. I feel very sorry for that poor young lad after all his efforts. Twas his pride and joy.'

'Did you know him well?' asked Bill.

'Sure I got to know him,' said Cornelius. 'I got to know him as well as you can know any stranger. A lovely young man. Very well mannered. Clever too.'

'Really,' said Bill.

'Christ yes,' said Cornelius, 'he was a mine of information. Knew about all kinds of buildings out foreign. He learnt to thatch since he came over here. The bloody man could turn his hand to anything.'

'I'd say now Cornelius you showed him a thing or two yourself,' said Keohane. And then he said to Bill: 'Cornelius here is one of the finest tradesmen in this part of the country.'

'Good for you,' said Bill

Cornelius took a sip of his whiskey and then turned to look at Bill. 'By all accounts you did great work to rescue him last night.'

'I happened to be in the right place at the right time,' said Bill. 'I was driving west on the Bantry Line. I was somewhere out near Coosán Gap when I saw this bright light away south. At first I thought it was a low-flying aeroplane until I got nearer. I could see the flames after awhile. I must have been three or four miles away.'

'Lucky you knew the lie of the land,' said Cornelius

'I hadn't been over those little by-roads for thirty years,' said Bill, 'but I had a fairly good notion where I was going.'

'If you were a city man you were lost for sure, but once knowing it you'd never forget.' Cornelius drank again. So did Bill. Keohane watched and listened.

'So you learned a bit about this man?' said Bill.

'Ah, he told me a few things about his background alright. It seems his mother and father came from Ireland, Cork as a matter of fact, but he was adopted out in America when he was only very young.'

'That's a sad story,' said Bill, 'and what was he doing here?'

'He came back looking for them. He has a notion they're still alive and living here somewhere.'

'Well, I hope he finds them,' said Bill.

'What's the news on his condition?' asked Cornelius.

'The paper said he was seriously injured,' said Keohane.

'He didn't look that bad to me,' said Bill, 'the ambulance man said he had only minor burns, but you never can tell. I'm driving down to Bantry to see him now.'

'Are you faith?' asked Cornelius.

'Yes,' said Bill, 'would you like to come along?'

'I'd like to go, but I'm sure you'd rather go on your own,' said Cornelius modestly.

'Not at all,' said Bill. 'On the contrary I'd be glad of some company.'

'Fair enough, I'll go so,' said Cornelius.

'Ready when you are then,' said Bill. 'Knock that back.'

They drained their glasses and stood up.

'Are you around for long?' asked Keohane.

'Until I get to the bottom of this business anyway,' said Bill. 'I'll have to give a statement to the Sergeant later on. So it all depends.'

'Well done again,' said Keohane, 'and I hope that lad is going to recover in short order.'

'We'll soon find out,' said Bill.

CHAPTER 11

downstream with the flood

When Joey arrived back at his house it was mid-afternoon. He saw two cars pulled up in front. One was a Gárda squad car and the other was unmarked. His mouth went dry and his heart began to pound in his chest like a jackhammer. At the same time his palms became sweaty and he felt a strange sensation in his stomach like an injection of some substance into his guts that caused him to go weak at the knees. My God, someone had acted fast. His mind began to race furiously. He wasn't ready for this at all. He'd have to buy time somehow. He'd have to bluff it out. He got out of his car slowly and Sergeant Sheridan, sitting in the passenger seat regarded him laconically: 'Hello, Joey,' he said.

'Sergeant,' said Joey desperately trying to be nonchalant and cheerful, yet inwardly shaking life a leaf.

What would he do? Go over and talk to them or casually go into the house? He opted for the latter.

'Grand day,' said the Sergeant.

'Spring has sprung,' said Joey and continued walking. After all this is what they'd expect from him. Drunk, Joey might fawn over the Guards. A sober Joey would be somewhat distant with them. So he followed form.

The Sergeant smiled a cold half-smile at his driver beside him and got out. The car behind them had two plain-clothes detectives sitting smoking. The Sergeant went over to them. They looked tough and grim-faced as if they'd shoot you dead at a whim. 'Leave this to me for a minute,' said the Sergeant.

They strolled casually towards the house, looking around all the while. As the Sergeant's shadow darkened the door, Joey was standing at the large oak table trying with trembling hands to open up his laptop. The Sergeant and the other Gárda walked in. They looked idly around. Joey continued to stare at his computer screen, studiously avoiding the Sergeant's gaze. He was having to keep himself upright by holding onto the leaf of the table. Christ, he hoped they didn't notice. But he'd have to brazen this out, go on the offensive. Only way. The Sergeant cleared his throat and Joey said: 'Make yourself at home Sergeant, seeing as how you've invited yourself in anyway. Not that you needed inviting. My door is always open.'

'Indeed,' said the Sergeant, 'I know that.'

'You could come in here any time you liked. In fact somebody was in already while I was away I notice.'

'How do you know that?' asked the Sergeant. Joey

looked at the Sergeant then down at the screen. He
wasn't seeing what was on it. He was trying to think. He
took a deep breath and thought he'd have to somehow
blind them with science. Throw them off the scent.

'Well, Sergeant, there was this particular note that I
had placed on a certain spot on the table before I left; on
a hot spot if you like. This was identifiable to no one
save myself. Now this message was for a friend of mine
named Rita, whom I believe you know.'

'No I don't,' said the Sergeant curtly.

'Didn't I ask you to phone her the last time you were
here?' asked Joey, 'and very civil of you too,' he added
lamely.

'So?'

'The note was moved. Here it is on spot 'B' but I
placed it on spot 'A' over there.' And Joey moved the
note to the original location: 'Now the only deduction
any person of even passing mathematical or analytical
ability could make is that the note was either moved:
one, by somebody or, two, that it moved by itself.
Certainly either of these alternatives is a possibility.
Alternative one is a possibility as my door is always
unlocked, *vide* your own means of entry. Alternative two
is also a possibility should a light zephyr disturb the
afternoon tranquility and blow the note across the table.
The note is light and would offer little resistance to even
a small breeze. However I have to discount that second
theory immediately in this instance as the note was held
in place and firmly wedged underneath this rather heavy
paperweight.'

My God, what gobbledy-gook. How was he doing? He

hardly knew what he was saying at this point. The scene was becoming a little unreal in its intensity. He somehow managed to produce a glass paperweight in the shape of an oval at one side and flat on the bottom, beautifully coloured with greens and greys and blues. He blundered on. 'You see, this rather lovely object depicting the desert sands of the Mojave under a midnight-blue sky, blown in glass for me by an artist out in Malibu whose name escapes me…ah sweet Malibu, sometimes I wish I'd stayed there…anyway this was the instrument of detention for the aforementioned note. It couldn't have moved unless somebody moved the paperweight. *Ergo,* I had a visitor unbeknownst to me in the past seventy two hours. Now it could have been the lovely Rita, for whom I left the note, telling her I would be in Kinsale for the next several days, but if she was here she would invariably have taken the note or thrown it in the fire once read. That is her usual *modus operandi.* So in short I believe it must have been someone else. The Sergeant's eyes were beginning to narrow in suspicion and irritation. He was surely on to his smokescreen? He tried to ask with exaggerated deference: 'Can I offer you something, Frank, a cup of tea maybe?'

The Sergeant smoothed his moustache and declined the offer: 'No,' he said coldly, 'but I would like to ask you a few questions.'

'Fire away,' said Joey. 'And please take a seat.' He sat down himself, almost flopped down. The effort of keeping up appearances taking a severe toll. Could the Sergeant see the thin line of sweat on his upper lip? The Sergeant took off his peaked cap and laid it carefully on the upright of a chair. He sat down and said: 'You know why we're here don't you?'

'No, Sergeant, as a matter of fact I do not. Though the presence of two plainclothes officers in your accompanying car suggests it's nothing trivial.' The Sergeant shifted in his seat and produced the morning paper: 'You've seen this I expect?'

'Several hours ago,' said Joey. 'And I've heard the contents on every hourly news bulletin on the radio to boot.'

'We have reason to suspect you may have had a hand in this.'

Joey sat back and scratched his head: 'What, in burning the thatched cottage?'

'Yes,' said the Sergeant.

'And what evidence do you have?'

'We have a number of reasons.'

'You have?' Joey looked from one to the other. Think you poltroon, think.

'Your attitude in general to newcomers in this town and in particular your outburst some months ago against the young man whose house was burnt down causes us to identify you as the prime suspect.'

'You mean my encounter with various parties at the Urban District Council meeting?'

'Exactly. You offered violence to this young man at that meeting.'

'On the contrary,' said Joey indignantly, suddenly clutching at a straw to fight with. 'I did no such thing. I called him a lot of interesting names of an insulting nature, I told him he was full of excrement, and I called his mother a whore. But I did not offer him violence.'

'I have the word of several people who will say otherwise.'

'Look, Sergeant,' said Joey, 'these meetings carry what they call a transcript. A secretary or a stenographer takes down everything that was said. In fact at this meeting I believe everything was taped. All you have to do is play the recording back. You'll hear angry words from me, yes. You'll hear vehement argument, shouting, swearing even; but that is not tantamount to threatening somebody, nor is it evidence.'

'I know you're a lawyer,' said the Sergeant, 'but you won't blind me with science here. You can parse all you like but your bullshit doesn't fool me.'

'I'm not trying to fool you, Sergeant. I'm trying to defend myself against an allegation of arson.'

'Apart from the meeting, I have information from a man at another location that day that you threatened dire consequences for this American.'

'Who's that?' Joey tried to put on a sneering tone.

'Jim Keohane.'

'Jim Keohane, that two-faced *Tadgh a dá thaobh?*'

'Jim Keohane is a dependable man in this town, call him what you like.'

'Dependable in what way? Dependable to sell you Guards liquor after hours on the qt?' And Joey threw his head back and tried to laugh one of his loud, cackling laughs which on this occasion petered out into a hoarse whimper. The Sergeant looked at his assistant and they exchanged glances suggesting they'd had enough of Joey's attempted stonewalling.

'That's enough, Joey. We have other information that

we're not going to disclose to you right now. We're going to have to ask you to come with us.'

'Where?'

'To the station. You can come peacefully or we can bring some reinforcements who may not be as gentle as John here and myself.'

Joey was shaking. The bead of sweat on his upper lip had spread to his forehead, and was spreading like saddlebags under his armpits. He thought he was finally going to faint. The young driver, John, took him by the arm.

'Aren't you forgetting something?' asked Joey trying to recover his composure but his heart felt like lead in his shoes.

'What's that?' asked the Sergeant.

'That note of which I spoke; the one under the paperweight.'

The Sergeant picked it up and read it. He reached for a pouch and put the note into it: 'All this note says is that you were going to Kinsale. It could have been written to put people off the scent. I'm afraid this doesn't prove where you were last night. You'll need a better alibi than that.'

Joey walked out in front of them and blinked in the bright light. The peaceful Ilen flowed down to the sea before their eyes. The white-budded blackthorn seemed several shades whiter; the day more beautiful than ever. Joey sighed as he sat into the back of the squad car. One of the plainclothes men sat in the back beside him. The Sergeant and John, the driver sat in front. Suddenly Joey seemed like a frail, vulnerable stick of a man in his loose and crumpled tweed suit. The two cars moved slowly up the narrow road along a winding inlet of the Ilen's wide estuary. Seagulls and gannets screamed and dived for fish. Kittiwakes flew over the flowing tide. A rowboat with six oarsmen went downstream with the flood.

CHAPTER 12

the desert's edge

The hospital was hushed and peaceful. The injured George Conklin lay sleeping in a room with north-facing windows, commanding spectacular views of Bantry Bay and the mountains of Glengariff and the Beara Peninsula in the distance. A variety of drips and other attachments were entangled from a wheeled trolley to his body. Bill and Cornelius sat quietly in two chairs provided by the helpful matron, watching his chest rise and fall, and listening to his quiet breathing. When they first arrived George was awake although quite groggy and Cornelius had introduced Bill as the man who had rescued him the previous night. George was overwhelmed with gratitude for Bill's efforts but couldn't remember a whole lot about the evening apart from the fact that he'd been visiting with some neighbours down the hill near the yellow schoolhouse. He vaguely remembered seeing the building

blazing before his eyes as he returned around midnight
and he must have dashed in to try to salvage some
belongings. When Bill explained that he found him
halfway down the stairs George said that was the last
memory he had until he woke up in the hospital this
morning. They chatted some more and George's eyes
began to glaze over a little. He sighed and asked: 'Is it
gone, the entire thing?'

'I'm afraid it is,' said Cornelius.

George heaved another sigh and looked out the
window. He didn't appear to take comfort from the blue
mountains today. He'd looked sad. Cornelius reached
over and took his hand. 'No matter, Georgie boy,' he
said, 'you're alive, that's all that matters.' He'd held onto
his hand for some minutes. George seemed to derive
solace from his touch. He looked quietly at Cornelius.
He'd appeared calmer. The matron had come in and said
perhaps the young man shouldn't talk for too much
longer. He'd had a severe trauma but thankfully nothing
life-threatening. He'd be able to leave in a few days, all
going well. They could talk some more later. Bill and
Cornelius had gone out for lunch and now were back. It
was late afternoon. The shadows were painting new
shapes on the mountains far away: Glenlough,
Knockowen, Hungry Hill.

George awoke some minutes after they returned and
sat up slowly. Cornelius stood up and walked over to
him. 'Do you want anything?' he asked. George's eyes
began to focus slowly, taking stock of the room.

'Maybe a drop of water from that jug,' he said.
Cornelius filled a glass with water and handed it to

George. He drank deeply. Bill smiled over at him. 'You look a good deal better,' he said. 'How do you feel?'

'Sore,' said George, 'but I'm in one piece thanks to you.'

'Well, you should try to relax and enjoy our Irish hospitality,' said Bill.

'The nurses are wonderful,' said George, 'so patient and considerate.'

'They say the Irish make the best nurses,' said Cornelius. 'I hear there's fierce demand for them in America.'

'There is,' said George, 'I can see why.' He took another sip of his water and there was silence until Bill said: 'Cornelius tells me you're from California. What part?'

'L.A.' said George, 'do you know it?'

'As a matter of fact I do,' said Bill. 'I lived there at one stage when I was younger.'

'Really,' said George.

'I lived in Santa Monica,' said Bill, 'and Malibu. I also spent some time in San Francisco.'

'A beautiful city,' said George.

'Yes,' said Bill, 'but as a matter of fact I liked Los Angeles even more.'

'Really.'

'There was something I loved about the sun and the freeways. The dry desert air and the palm trees. It's an extraordinary place. Something new happening every day.'

'I know what you mean,' said George.

'Where were you brought up?' asked Bill.

'A number of places, said George. 'I believe I was born in the hospital in Santa Monica. My mother was from Ireland, but I don't remember her. My father too but they separated. She had me adopted soon after I was born. I was brought up by a couple named Conklin out in the high desert.'

'And what brings you to Ireland?

'Curiosity about my origins I guess was the main reason. The second reason was to get away from California. It's become very crowded and dangerous. I was telling Cornelius here all about it.'

'You were faith,' said Cornelius, 'and it sounds like a mighty fine place altogether to me. Sure how can you stick the weather here after all that glorious sunshine?'

'The weather isn't everything,' said George.

'I remember the weather,' said Bill, 'although it's nearly thirty years since I lived there. You never forget the weather.'

'Have you been back since?' asked George

'On business only, not to live.'

'And why did you leave it originally?'

'You know, that's a good question,' said Bill. 'I was very happy there in my early twenties. The living was easy. I was searching for myself I guess. Young men are restless. You should know that.'

'Sure do,' said George.

'Well, I'm sorry your welcome here wasn't better,' said Bill. 'It was a disgrace to burn your cottage. I'm ashamed to think an Irishman may have done it.'

'Ah, sure maybe 'twas an accident,' said Cornelius, 'though I doubt it.'

'Unlikely to be an accident,' said George. 'You know how well we built that cottage, Cornelius. It was virtually fire-proof unless done deliberately. What are the police saying?'

'They're investigating,' said Bill. 'but it's too soon to say. I'm due to talk to them later and I'll let you know what they say. But I expect they'll talk to yourself directly anyway in a day or two.'

'There's rumours going round of course,' said Cornelius.

'About who?' asked George.

'Well, we shouldn't be saying this but you remember that fellow who attacked you at the meeting?'

'What was his name again?' asked George.

'Harrison,' said Bill, 'Joey Harrison. I'm shocked if it's him. I'll have to confront him. I find it hard to believe it could be true.'

'You know him?' asked George, surprised.

'For forty years,' said Bill. 'As a matter of fact he was in California with me. He's gone a bit bitter in recent years. Hopefully he didn't do this. It's not like him at all to do something like this.'

'Of course rumours are dangerous things,' said Cornelius. 'Rumours can hang a man with no proof.'

'Don't I know,' said Bill. He looked out the window and thought momentarily of last week's newspaper headlines. It was a funny old world. Did George and Cornelius know about them he wondered? Unlikely if George would relate to them. Cornelius maybe. But he'd be much too polite to say anything. He'd always think the best of Bill although not being personally acquainted with him before now. But he probably knew his father in the old days.

'Did you know my father?' Bill asked Cornelius suddenly, 'Tom Cassidy?'

'Tom Cassidy? Why wouldn't I have known Tom Cassidy?' said Cornelius. 'Tom Cassidy was a great fighting man. He fought in the old brigade you know.'

'I know that,' said Bill.

'You're well got to have had a father like Tom Cassidy,' said Cornelius.

'Your father was a soldier?' asked George of Bill.

'He fought in the old revolution,' said Bill.

'He fought to free Ireland,' said Cornelius. 'Back in the early twenties. I remember him although I was a young lad. He was a hero.'

'Wow,' said George, 'that's a nice heritage.'

'It is,' said Bill. 'he was a better man than I'll ever be.' Bill was suddenly silent, thinking back through all the vanished years, lost and never to return. Thinking of his own vainglorious pursuit of money and fame, and the people who had loved him but whom he'd left behind.

The nurse came back and Bill stood up. 'I think we'd better let this young man rest up, Cornelius,' he said. Cornelius stood up.

'You're right,' he said, 'we're only talking nonsense here anyway.'

'I really appreciate you coming,' said George.

'What will you do now?' asked Bill. 'When you recover I mean.'

'I really don't know,' said George, 'I really don't know.' He looked lost. His eyes looked haunted for the briefest of moments and then the moment was gone. He was a man who had a firm grip on his emotions.

'Does your stepfather know what happened?' asked Bill.

'Not yet,' said George, 'but I intend to call him in a day or two when I'm back on my feet.'

'Keep in touch,' said Bill. And he reached inside his pocket for a business card. 'Here's my card,' he said. 'If there's anything I can do to help please give me a call.'

'Thanks very much,' said George, 'I really appreciate it.'

Bill shook his hand. He held it for a moment and thought what a warm and pleasant and strong young man he was.

As they drove back in silence over the side of Mount Gabriel and down into Schull they could see all the islands golden in the sunset: Long Island, Horse Island, Castle Island. 'That's a beautiful sight,' said Cornelius.

'It never fails to take my breath away,' said Bill. They descended by winding turns and Bill said, 'George is a fine young man.'

'He'll be alright,' said Cornelius. 'He's got his feet on the ground.'

'Still, he'll be in shock. And he has no one here. No relatives.'

'I wonder who his parents are?' said Cornelius, 'or if they're still alive?'

'I was wondering about that too,' said Bill. 'It's kind of a sad story.'

'I hope he finds them,' said Cornelius eventually.

'I hope so,' said Bill.

The sun shone with a brilliant spring blue. Boats of all shapes and sizes were being put to sea after winter hibernation. The ubiquitous tourists were coming out of the woodwork on the main street. The early swallows shrieked and swooped out over the harbour. Yet Bill could not concentrate on all this effulgent flowering. His mind was back in those early carefree days beside the wide Pacific. He could still recall the peculiar, sweet comforting smell of poinsetta, jacaranda and bougainvillea. Sweeter after rain. And rain so rare a wonder. And the music, the aching romantic music of The Doors, The Grateful Dead and Jefferson Airplane:

"Do you want somebody to love,
Do you need somebody to love…"

And Eileen, oh Eileen, kissing him goodbye out on the desert's edge and the shadow of Joey lurking somewhere in the background. She looking particularly beautiful and glowing with an inner serenity. And then a furtive tear glassing her brown eyes, her light summer dress rising like a small protective sail around her knees. And then the roar of a beat-up old Chevy Impala engine and a cloud of dust. And the wave of a coloured handkerchief as the burning sun hid behind a stray cloud. And a blue jay or hawk or bald eagle hovered in the air.

CHAPTER 13

the code of silence

'You could be charged with attempted murder you know,' said Sergeant Sheridan.

'You're trying to intimidate me, Frank,' said Joey, though the fear was very real in his eyes. Joey was sitting at a cold aluminium table in a sparsely furnished Garda station. There were no adornments of any kind. The walls needed painting. The room was dark with one dirty window letting in meagre light and this required a single, one hundred watt bulb to be left alight. It dangled from the ceiling with no shade to render it less harsh. There were two other people in the room as well as the Sergeant and these were the two plainclothes Special Branch detectives Joey had already encountered at his house. One was standing behind Joey so that he had to turn around to reply to him whenever he spoke and the other was sitting on a plastic chair opposite him and beside the Sergeant. Joey felt cold and lonely and hungry. The only sustenance provided was a large jug of cold water with a bunch of plastic cartons, which everybody helped themselves to from time to time. All except Joey. His rations were doled out parsimoniously by the detective. He'd been here now for at least six hours. He was hungry and thirsty. He was very tired. They'd read him his rights when they brought him in and the shame he felt at being recognized by many onlookers was hard to bear. Then he'd been put in a cell smelling of vomit and urine and stale beer for about two hours, until they brought him into this other equally depressing and forbidding star chamber. Oh, yes, they knew how to deal you the cards when the chips were down. They made you feel small, helpless and extremely vulnerable and that was ever before the fun began.

'Intimidating you?' asked the Sergeant. 'If you think this is intimidation you've seen nothing yet. No, my dear Joey, as a matter of fact I'm trying to be as nice to you as I possibly can in view of the standing of you and your family in this community and the number of years we both have been acquainted. But make no mistake, arson is a very serious crime. If that young man dies, then, needless to say, you are in very deep shit indeed. If he doesn't you are still in big trouble. If you make our lives a little easier and admit to this whole thing, then we will take that into consideration at your trial, or should I say the judge will. If you don't co-operate, we'll throw the book at you. It's your choice.'

Joey's mind worked furiously. He had an alibi but how could he explain his situation to Corinne? He'd created a false image of himself to her and perhaps she wouldn't co-operate now when she heard of his arrest. He'd have to divulge his *mal fides*. My God, what a mess. And again the shame. Joey Harrison arrested and locked up. What of his modest but solid position in this community, where everybody had his place? The butcher, the baker, the candlestick maker; the corner-boy, the bank manager, the chairman of the hurling club. And the creator of public opinions, the seer, the intellectual: he himself, Joseph Arden Harrison? The more he considered it the greater the indignity seemed to appear. Was a man not entitled to express an opinion? To stand for something?

Joey said: 'You think, Frank, because I hold certain views that it follows, *ipso facto*, that I must be somehow responsible for the fallout from the vociferous expression of those views. You know, it became fashionable in the eighties to typecast anybody who expressed an Irish Nationalist point of view or who even supported the Irish Language as a Provisional IRA fellow traveller. For Christ's sake, what did our forebears fight for except to enable us to say our piece without fear or favour?'

'Your forebears would *not* have been in favour of burning someone out,' said the Sergeant.

'On the contrary,' said Joey, 'it became their strongest weapon of retaliation. Lord Bandon was burnt out, Castlefreake, and scores of other spies and collaborators. Only, I might add, after, and here's a statistic to grapple with, only after forty-six thousand homes were burnt to the ground by the Black and Tans in the province of Munster. But the virtue of retaliation by fire soon put a stop to the gallop of the Tans.'

'This is no time for a history lesson,' said the standing detective, 'especially from someone like you.'

Joey turned slowly around. He finally decided to shrug off his fear and confront these bastards. 'And what pray, would you know about history?' he said with a sneer. 'Since when has a member of the Special Branch ever held a point of view other than one conducive to keeping his paymasters in power and feathering his own nest?'

'Shut your mouth or we'll shut it for you,' said the sitting detective. He had a plain face like an overfed bullock, crew-cutted and ample-chinned. Joey decided a history lesson was certainly lost on him.

'Where were you last night? I'll ask you one last time?' said the standing detective, hovering over Joey with a mean and cobra-like stare in his slit eyes.

'Alright then, you want to know where I was last night? I'll tell you where,' said Joey. And he sat upright, straightened his tie and buttoned his jacket. 'I was in the arms of a beautiful woman.'

The Sergeant and his two abettors stopped and stared at Joey. Then they looked at each other. Then the Sergeant looked back at Joey and smiled incredulously: 'Look Joey, if this is another one of your fantasies drop it right now. This is deadly serious.'

'So am I,' said Joey and added, 'would you like to know the damsel's name?'

'Yes we would.'

'Her name is Corinne Daly.'

'From where?'

'From Kinsale, via South County Dublin.'

'And you were with this lady last night?'

'Last night of all,' said Joey triumphantly.

The two detectives ground their lower mandibles with the disappointed expressions of two people who have been cheated out of a very starry prize. Sergeant Frank Sheridan stroked his large, black moustache, stared balefully at Joey and wondered what to say next. Without changing his po-faced expression he asked in a low monotone that had lost its earlier certainty: 'How can you prove this?'

'A simple phone call should confirm it,' said Joey, 'but I'm afraid the State will have to foot the cost of that.'

'There's the phone,' said the Sergeant.

'I'll have to check the number,' said Joey, 'excuse me a moment.' He gave a fake, apologetic smile as he took out a dog-eared diary from his inside pocket. Then he took the phone and dialled laboriously. He put the speaker to his ear and stared unblinkingly at his tormentors. The number kept ringing without a response. The Sergeant pressed the loudspeaker button for all to hear. Suddenly a voice said hello at the other end. It was deep, hoarse and husky: Corinne unmistakably. 'Corinne?' asked Joey.

'That's me,' said the husky voice.

'Corinne, this is Joey.'

'Joey, how are you?' She sounded pleased but not wildly enthusiastic. 'I've been thinking about you.'

'No need to lie to make me feel better,' said Joey.

'No, really,' she said, her tone warming. 'I wanted to thank you for the carnations. They're beautiful. So thoughtful of you.' Joey smiled a tight-lipped, sardonic, told-you-so smile at his inquisitors who shifted on their seats and looked slightly embarrassed.

'Did you get home alright?' continued Corinne.

'Oh, yes, I had a pleasant drive until I arrived back here. Then the shit hit the fan.'

'What do you mean?' she asked.

'Did you not hear the news?'

'No, I've been so busy catching up...'

'Well, you should, because your boss is all over the papers once again.'

'Bill? What's happened now?' She sounded crest-fallen.

'Oh, it's good news this time,' said Joey brightly. 'He saved a man from a burning house last night, on the side of Owen mountain.'

'Bill Cassidy?'

'The same.'

'Where's Owen mountain?'

'In darkest West Cork.'

'What's he doing in West Cork? I thought he was stuck in that Tribunal in Dublin, as we discussed?'

'So did I, but the wheel of fortune turns my dear, and quickly too.'

Corinne was silent for a few moments, then she said: 'That's amazing, I can't believe it.'

'Neither can I. Now that's the good news. The bad news is that I've been arrested and accused of setting this house on fire. It was a thatched house incidentally,' he finished dryly.

'You've been... oh my God, this gets weirder and weirder, how could you have burnt it when you were here with me?'

'My point entirely,' said Joey, 'but I have some Spanish Inquisition types here who seem to think I have the gift of bilocation.'

'Who do you mean, the police?'

'Yes.'

'Joey, is this one of your little April fool jokes or something?' said Corinne, suddenly sounding anxious. 'If it is I don't think it's funny.'

The Sergeant grabbed the phone from Joey and spoke into the receiver: 'Neither do we Ms…?'

'Daly, Corinne Daly. Who's this?'

'Thank you, Ms. Daly. This is Sergeant Frank Sheridan of the West Cork Garda Serious Crimes Squad. You heard what Mr. Harrison has said, and the purpose of this call is for you to establish Mr. Harrison's alibi for last night. May I ask you a few questions?'

'Yes, sir, I mean Sergeant, of course,' said Corinne, suddenly quiet and subdued, her voice reduced to almost a whisper for a moment.

'You were with Mr. Harrison as you say. Where?'

'Well, first of all we were out for dinner at the Man Friday restaurant in Kinsale.'

'For how long?'

'Approximately three hours from eight o'clock till eleven.'

'And then?'

'And then…?'

'Yes, where did you go then?'

'Well, we went back to Mr. Harrison's suite of rooms.'

'Mr. Harrison had a suite of rooms?' asked the surprised Sergeant.

'Yes, in the Jamesfort Hotel. He was here for about five days altogether.'

'I see.' The Sergeant kept looking from his colleagues to Joey with an ever more bewildered look on his face.

'And what happened then?'

'How do you mean exactly, Sergeant?'

'I mean where did you go next?'

'Nowhere, we spent the night together.' The husky tone was back in Corinne's voice.

'Let me get this straight, Ms Daly. You're telling me that Mr. Harrison spent five days in one of the most expensive hotels in Ireland, that he had a suite of rooms there, and that you spent the entire night with him in that suite of rooms last night?'

'That's correct,' said Corinne sweetly.

'What was Mr. Harrison doing at the Jamesfort Hotel in the first place?'

'He was investigating Bill Cassidy's affairs.'

'He was what?'

'Yes, he was working for *The Chronicle* newspaper, doing a piece of investigative journalism for them. I presume they paid his expenses.'

'What?' Joey's exclamation escaped from his lips in spite of himself. 'How did you know that, Corinne?' he shouted above the Sergeant's voice.

'Oh, it was pretty obvious to me after a day or two that you were more than a visiting lawyer. I figured you were a reporter in the end Joey. I was convinced when you paid for dinner last night with a credit card supplied by the newspaper. You see, working in publicity I get to

see and meet all kinds of people. I've become fairly good
at figuring out who's who and what's what.'

'Well of all the…' Joey was speechless. The Sergeant
handed him back the phone. Joey grabbed it up. It was
still on loudspeaker.

'My God, Corinne, it's you who should be the
detective. You had me taped all along?'

'My dear Joey, you're more easily read than you
realize. Of course I had you taped. You're such a softie
really, Joey, the hard facade you like to put on is not
really you is it?'

'Well blow me down,' said Joey. 'Listen Corinne,
you've saved my ass here. How can I thank you enough
for everything?'

'No need to thank me, Joey. I had so much fun. You
taught me so much and you know, you really are the
most wonderful lover.' Her bewitching voice was now
like a Senorina's calling to her Latin lover across the
streets of Naples as the sun set on the Isle of Capri.

The Sergeant sputtered the water from the plastic cup
he had been drinking all over the desk. The two
detectives looked totally at sixes and sevens. The
Sergeant grabbed the phone: 'Gimme that,' he said to
Joey. Then he said to Corinne: 'Ms Daly, you've been
most helpful to us in our investigations. You have
provided an alibi for Mr. Harrison which we will be
relying upon. Now, any further intimate conversations
between you two will have to be conducted at the
expense of either *The Chronicle* or the Jamesfort Hotel,
but not at the expense of An Gárda Síochána. Thank you
again and good day to you. We will be in touch again.'

And he put the phone down. He sat back in his chair and held his hands under his chin, fingertips touching. He wrinkled his exasperated brow and cogitated. Joey looked back at him like an arch child who has gotten away with eating all the biscuits yet again without censure. 'So, what have we here?' the Sergeant said at last, 'a fucking Casanova *and* a Bob Woodward, all rolled into one.'

'Swearing doesn't become you, Frank,' said Joey, suddenly back to his flippant best. The Sergeant nodded his head ruefully and said. 'You may have gotten away with it this time Joey, but sooner or later I'll catch you out. I'd stake my life on it that you are mixed up in this somehow, but as of now I can't prove it. But don't get too smug. You'll trip yourself up sooner or later and when you do I'll be waiting for you. We know you're the real Provo sympathizer around here, not Bill Cassidy. That part never made sense to me.'

'At least we agree on one thing Sergeant,' said Joey.

The Sergeant stood up. As Joey stood he turned to the Sergeant and said: 'You know Frank there are wheels within wheels. You think you know everything about this community but you don't. First of all, let me say that it has never been Provo policy to hound well-meaning and friendly foreigners out of Ireland. Especially Americans. The Provos go after a different type of client altogether and always have done. As you say, I know quite a few of them and to me this does not look like their style of operation at all, at all. Perhaps you should be searching under some other rocks besides the obvious ones.'

'Well who do you suggest then?'

'That's your job, Frank. Perhaps we'll never know. The code of silence is a long and venerated custom in old Ireland, going back a long way, past the Whiteboys, the Fenians, the Peep O' Day Boys. But if I hear anything I'll let you know.' And Joey put his index finger to the side of his nose in a knowing signal as he headed for the door.

'Don't get too big for your boots, Joey,' said the Sergeant coldly as Joey walked out from the cool of the grim barracks and stood relieved in the magic light of sunset.

CHAPTER 14

palimpsest

One day in early June, Joey Harrison showed up at George Conklin's door at the old farmhouse in the shadow of Owen mountain. The roses were not yet in bloom, and the longest day was still a good ways off. It was one of those wet and windy mornings that occasionally hit the south coast of Ireland at this time of year rendering everything a washed-out colourless grey; one of those days beloved of certain artists in that locality who like to paint the dripping landscapes of the heart in pale blues and greys and anaemic reds, literally creating the effect of dripping by leaving their works out under the thunderheads that drift down from Owen and from Sheha. After twelve hours of this treatment nature has completed without effort or interference the image as originally conceived: a pale, drizzle-streaked diptych. George was talking to his Dutch neighbour, Rutger, who lived in a restored mill some miles away and Rutger was in the act of demonstrating his technique to George on this particular cloudy morning when Joey appeared unannounced. In the background the burnt out husk of the gorgeous thatched cottage stood as a sinister and sad reminder to man's capacity for precipitate and destructive action.

Joey had pulled his old Mercedes into the yard and as he got out slowly he noticed two men absorbed in some discussion over in front of the farmhouse door. He was spruce in his new-look, tweed suit and cravat: he'd decided the scruffy image became him no longer. He walked slowly around the front of the car and stood looking at the ruined thatch, forlorn in the rain. He shook his head in an exaggerated gesture of empathy and regret. The two men over at the farmhouse door continued to study the paintings and behaved as if there was nobody there. Joey walked over slowly and when he reached them he stood contemplating the line of paintings which Rutger had set up in a row with the rain falling steadily on them. Joey stood nodding sagely as he moved from one easel to the next: 'Interesting technique,' he remarked eventually, stroking his chin with his right hand. He really didn't have the foggiest notion what he was looking at; except it was just that: foggy.

George hadn't recognized him but that didn't matter. In the time-honoured custom of the countryside nothing was undertaken quickly or suddenly. The matter of a person's identity would eventually emerge in the course of conversation. It was bad manners to set about anything abruptly and these two obvious outsiders had clearly adapted seamlessly to the local ways. But Joey had recognized the young American straight away. It was good to see he was none the worse for wear. Thank God for that. Joey's new apparel probably disguised him effectively and he relaxed into the role of art connoisseur without further ado. 'What's it supposed to depict?' he asked as authoritatively as he could.

'That's a subjective matter,' said Rutger. 'It depicts whatever you think it depicts.' The accent was guttural, fluid and Dutch.

'Well I'm bound to say I'm at a loss,' said Joey. And he scratched his head.

'Mountains, can't you see mountains?' asked Rutger. These continentals were very direct.

'Damned if I can see any mountains,' said Joey, peering harder.

'It's an original technique,' said Rutger, 'I've devised it myself since I came to live in this climate. First you do the line drawing using dry pigment on paper. You draw what you see. In this case those beautiful mountains in front of your eyes.' He pointed to a part of the painting that Joey agreed could be construed as a mountain, at a pinch.

'It's like a watercolour,' said Rutger. 'Then when it rains, like today, I leave it out and you get the results that you see before you. Clear and austere.'

'Well, it does possess a certain attractiveness,' agreed Joey, 'but I like my mountains in the old fashioned way. I like a mountain to look like a mountain.'

Rutger shrugged the way only continentals can shrug and said: 'Hey, you draw mountains looking like mountains, after awhile it becomes boring. So I like to change it.'

'And how much are you asking for that?' asked Joey.

'For you, two thousand,' smiled Rutger.

'Euros?' asked Joey.

'Yes,' said Rutger.

'Ah, Jasus,' said Joey, 'who are you trying to kid?'

'You don't like it, try another,' said Rutger. Joey walked down the serried lines of easels once again: 'They all look the same to me,' he said.

'You got a big house?' asked Rutger, 'these paintings need a lot of space.'

'I've got a big house alright,' said Joey, 'but a small pocketbook. I'm afraid your prices are too rich for my blood. But I know a man with deep pockets who might like to buy some. I'll tell him about you.'

Then Joey turned to look at George who'd been saying nothing: 'Don't I know you?' asked George.

'Joey Harrison by name,' Joey extended his hand. George shook it though not firmly and his eyes looked wary. He said: 'What brings *you* up here?' Joey pondered this question and then replied: 'Air is free, isn't it? I thought I'd come up to get some of the fresh variety.' Joey was, as usual, a ticklish customer. If you said black, Joey would always say white. It was his way of being in the world. 'Plenty of that up here, but more of rain' said Rutger. He smiled and his moustache stretched until the distance between its pointy ends and his ears was minimal. Joey looked at Rutger with a sardonic air but spoke to George. 'I wonder if we could have a word in private. Leave El Greco here to his triptychs?'

George hesitated and looked Joey up and down. The man sure had some neck. 'Alright then,' he said, 'go on in. I'll be there in a minute.'

'Fine,' said Joey. Before he walked in he said with a chuckle to Rutger: 'If you don't mind I'll take a rain check on those paintings of yours.'

As his guffaw floated out the open door he could hear Rutger say to Joey in his clipped, broken English: 'What is this, some kind of joker character?'

Joey looked around the traditional farmhouse kitchen. George had retained the great, blackened, open fireplace with the hobs for sitting on at either side. A turf fire burned low in an iron grate. The smell of burning turf was sweet and pungent. It carried Joey back to the age of eight or nine when he went as a schoolboy to his friend Bill Cassidy's farmhouse for snap-apple night. He used to like it so much better than his own grander but colder home near the town. He noticed the linoleum-covered pine table, the long clevvy over the fireplace displaying empty biscuit tins, tea caddies, coffee jars. Instead of a fridge George kept his food the old fashioned way in a safe. This was a tall, slender, rudimentary cabinet of plain wood with fine mesh wire covering the door. On the inside shelving he kept the bread, sugar, flour and tea on the top; meat, eggs, and tomatoes on the next shelf. Carrots, turnips, potatoes and cabbage filled the third shelf, and on the bottom shelf reposed the milk and cheese: this being the coolest section, nearest the stone-flagged floor. This young man was clearly a neat and organized individual, a typical American: they learned discipline, self-control and self-sufficiency at an early age.

A black, iron crane swung over the low fire and a large round pot called a bastible hung suspended from it. The bastible was specifically designed for baking soda bread and sure enough, as Joey lifted the lid he beheld inside the rising dough, turning a nice honey-brown colour. This would, in a matter of a half an hour, metamorphose into the delicious, thick, butter-flavoured cake the locals called without irony, *brown George*. It looked to be well on its way, swelling to a perfect tilth. Joey's eyes observed a self-sufficient world without the need of a television, radio or land line telephone. He was quite intrigued. As George came in at last Joey said: 'You have a beautiful place here. All the farmhouses looked like this in the old days. It brings back happy memories. I wonder where all the modern gadgets have got us when you see a cosy place like this?'

George thanked him and stood waiting expectantly. Joey said: 'Let me tell you why I came up here.'

'Sure,' said George, 'have a seat. Would you like some tea?'

'A cup in the hand would go down nicely.'

As George unhooked the bastible and hung the kettle on the crane, Joey continued: 'I expect you know who I am?'

'You're not exactly the most inconspicuous individual in these parts,' said George dryly, as he busied himself getting the teapot from the pine dresser and placing cups and saucers on the table. 'Right,' said Joey, 'and no doubt then you are aware of the rumours circulating about me and the fire?'

'That I am,' said George.

'Then, *a fortiori*, you're further aware that the police investigations against me have been abandoned.'

'So I hear,' said George.

'I had a perfect alibi. I was in Kinsale. I didn't do it.'

'So, why are you telling *me* all this?' asked George. The kettle had boiled. He scalded the teapot, then took the pot to the door and tossed the water away. 'You've learnt all the old skills,' said Joey, 'including the ancient art of wetting tea.'

'Thank you,' said George, 'but you didn't answer my question.'

'Oh, yes,' said Joey, 'well let's call it guilt for want of a better phrase. You see after our exchange of angry words at the UDC meeting perhaps some of those words were an incitement to some hotheads to take matters into their own hands. However, I can't be held responsible for other people's actions.'

'There are laws about incitement to hatred on the statute books.' said George.

'I don't think my words could be construed as incitement as such,' said Joey.

'Maybe, maybe, not,' said George. 'Anyway it's too late now. The damage is done.' George poured the tea. After both cups were filled Joey said: 'And nobody is sorrier than me about that damage, so the purpose of my visit is to see if I can make some reparation.'

'How?'

'I may be able to help you trace your parents.'

George put his cup down. 'You?' he said.

'Yes, absurd as it now may sound, in the light of things that have happened. However there are things about me that you don't know, and I've been doing some thinking about you and your situation. There are a number of strange coincidences that have occurred which have got me thinking back to the past. Come to think of it, they may not be coincidences at all but twists of fate or destiny, whatever you want to call them.'

'Sounds suitably vague,' said George with a hint of cynicism.

'Look, I don't want to get your hopes up,' said Joey, 'so I'm not going to divulge everything to you about my theory right now. But I know you're trying to find your Irish parents and I've been doing some research into it. You were brought up by the man who adopted you in California, right?'

'Right, my uncle Sam Conklin.'

'Is he still alive?'

'Yes, but what difference does it make?'

'You see, I used to live in California maybe around the time you were born. What year were you born?'

'Nineteen seventy-five.'

'I came back from California in seventy-five. What month were you born?'

'September.'

'Yes, yes, it could be connected.'

'What are you talking about?' asked George. Joey's sudden enthusiasm had him baffled.

'And have you told Uncle Sam all about your recent misfortunes, the fire and all that?' continued Joey as if he hadn't heard.

'Yes I have.'

'Do you think I could have a word with him?'

'What, on the phone?'

'You have a mobile phone don't you?'

'Why sure, but I don't see…'

'It's a hunch I have,' said Joey, 'I just want to ask him a few questions that may reveal something. It may be a waste of time, but it's worth a try.'

George was sceptical, but he'd been down a blind alley so far in his search, so while there was hope he would persist: 'Okay, then, here goes,' he said. He dialled the number on the mobile and Joey could hear it ringing faintly almost immediately. A voice answered: 'Sam Conklin here.'

'Uncle Sam, it's George.'

'Hey, Georgie boy, how ya' doin?' said Sam. 'How you been since?'

'On the mend.'

'Any news on the fire?'

'No, I'm afraid the police have hit a dead end on that so far.'

'What are your plans George, will you rebuild or come back home?'

'You know, Sam, I'm undecided about all that just now, but I have a man here who tells me he may be able to help me trace my parents.'

'Yeah, say, who's that?'

'A gentleman by the name of Harrison, Joey Harrison.'

'Never heard of him,' said Sam.

'He says he lived in California the year I was born. He may have some clues I could follow. He'd like a word with you.'

'Yeah, well, put him on.'

George handed the phone over to Joey: 'Hello, Mr. Conklin,' said Joey.

'Hi there, hi there,' said Sam.

'Look, Mr. Conklin, I'm sorry to say young George has gone through a lot of trauma over here, and I thought I may be able to help a little to get him sorted out.'

'Sure, sure,' said Sam, 'but you know, George is a top class fella. He'll do fine. And you know he's always welcome back to my house whenever he wants. It's all there for him anyway. I ain't gonna live forever.'

'You sound like a very generous man,' said Joey.

'What the hell,' said Sam, 'I do what I can. Life's too short and you can't take it with you.'

'You're right,' said Joey. 'But listen, I wondered if you had any way of tracing the names of George's blood parents?'

'No, no, that can't be done. You see part of the terms of adoption in this great state of California are that you're not given the names of the original parents. That's how it works see.'

'And are there no exceptions to that?' asked Joey.

'Hell, Mr. Harrison, there's exceptions to everything in life. I guess you're old enough yourself to have figured that out.'

'My point is,' said Joey, 'could you make an argument that in George's present circumstances an exception could be made?'

'Gee, I dunno,' said Sam, 'I've never been asked. You see George never asked me to do anything like that. Guess he didn't want to upset me or put me in second spot, but hell, yes I'd be glad to see what I could do.'

'You could make some enquiries then?' asked Joey.

'Well, I got some names of people who could make enquiries for me. Some people who know some senators and representatives over here. It's not orthodox you understand. But it could be done.'

'So you think you could trace the names.'

'I could try,' said Sam, 'couldn't guarantee anything.'

George asked Joey for the phone and spoke to Sam. 'Sorry to spring this on you Sam, it wasn't my idea though.'

'Oh, that's alright kid,' said Sam, 'but before I start running around like a headless chicken, tell me, this what's-his-name, Harrison, is he for real?' George smiled and looked at Joey and then said: 'I guess we've got to take him at face value. I guess it's straws in the wind, but listen, if it's too much trouble…'

'No, no kid, it's no trouble, anything I can do to help,' said Sam.

'Well you know all the politicians Sam, what about Senator Benson? Do you think we could go that route?'

'No, kid no, Benson's too official. We'd compromise him. But I'd go a different route, the union route.'

'The union route.'

'Yes, the Municipal Workers Union. I was a member for years. The people who are hands on, who keep the great state of California going on a day to day basis.'

'Well, if you think so…'

'Trust me on this George, this is the only way. Don't ask me too many details right now. Let me put my thinking cap on here. Put me back to Harrison will you.' George handed the phone back to Joey.

'Listen Mr. Harrison, maybe the mother's name. Maybe I could trace her name. I had some notion they weren't married you know. I didn't go into this too much with George. Didn't want to embarrass him you see.'

'Well, thank you, Mr. Conklin...'

'Sam, you can call me Sam.'

'Well, thank you Sam. One name is all I need, And you can keep this confidential by calling me back personally. Either it's the right name or else I'm barking up the wrong tree anyway. But if it is the right name, I mean the name I think it might be, then I can steer George to where he wants to go.'

'Sure, sure,' said Sam. 'Listen, just give me your address. I'll send you a letter. I like to do things the old-fashioned way. Keep it more formal. I'll write you in three or four weeks. It'll either work then or it won't.'

Joey gave Sam his address and then Joey thanked him and handed the phone back to George. George said goodbye to Sam and said maybe he was on to something at last. Sam wished him good luck said he'd look forward to coming over to Ireland if he hit pay dirt.

'He sounds like a nice man,' said Joey.

'He's the best,' said George, 'and his list of connections is as long as your arm. He knows everyone all over the United States in the Irish-American community. He has a great love for all things Irish. I believe he himself was raised by Catholic nuns who he says are the world's greatest people. He won't have anything bad said about them.'

'He has a point,' said Joey, 'the Church has become much maligned. All the fantastic work done over the years has been set to naught by some bad publicity. Me, myself I never bought into all that secular, politically correct, liberal shit. I'm like Sam. I like things the old-fashioned way.'

Joey stood up and said he'd better be going. George saw him to the door and Joey said that as soon as he got Sam's letter he'd be back to him one way or the other. He'd keep his fingers crossed.

As Joey drove back through the flat farmlands along the Ilen river, the rain suddenly cleared and the sun of June burst out hot and strong. The pollen count was heavy. All these new perennials grown by garden-proud householders: red, white and gold snapdragons, fragrant sweet Williams: causing his hay fever to kick in. His nose started running and his eyes became watery. Further along the farmers were busy with huge tractors cutting silage in the fields. No hay nowadays although the fever was still prevalent, notwithstanding. He was glad he had made the trip up to George. He was hoping to make amends. Bill Cassidy's stinging rebuke was still ringing in his ears from a few weeks ago, when he'd spoken on the phone to him. Bill had more or less accused him of getting some people to set the house on fire and no amount of protesting of innocence on Joey's part was going to change his mind. Bill had implied he had suborned arson by bribing some desperados to do the dirty work. What could Joey do? The stigma would probably live with him for a long time, but then, who doesn't have a stigma at the heel of the hunt? Let him without sin cast the first stone. There were a hell of a lot of hypocrites in Ireland with secrets to hide and what most delighted them was to find a scapegoat to lynch so they might expiate their guilt. Did Bill now think he himself was whiter than white with no flaws? And did he think Joey petty and jejune, consumed with local squabbles? But each personality, each character was an accumulation of actions both good and bad committed along life's pathway. A palimpsest, with only the latest writing visible to the world. Scratch beneath and what secrets were extant?

CHAPTER 15

a nest of vipers

Dublin lay basking in a hot June heatwave. All along the streets that ran in twisting clusters north and south of the Liffey, the stony-faced facades of winter were gone. Windows were thrown open and restaurant tables proliferated along the pavements under awnings. There was a languid, dreamy atmosphere, as music and accents from all over Europe drifted upwards in the soft summer air. Dublin city had gone continental. The rich were sailing their yachts out in Dublin Bay from Dun Laoghaire to Howth Head and those who worked for a living were looking forward to their chicken sandwiches at lunchtime, stretched out on the grass on St. Stephen's Green among the tulip and gladioli beds.

It was a little before eleven and Bill Cassidy was on his way to another encounter with his nemesis, Martha Williams, down by the Liffey side. As was his custom, he'd left his car at the depot in Sandyford and had taken the Luas tram into town, via Dundrum, Windy Arbour, and Ranelagh. Being back in Dublin brought the usual culture shock from which he never seemed to fully recover, despite thirty years of living in the city. What caused this malaise, this distemper of the soul? This deracination. Was it that his roots, ripped from the rough, hardy clay of Cork were never fully nourished in the lands inside the Pale? Always returning on the long road from Carberey his heart would start to falter. Usually around Cashel of the Kings, halfway from home. A hundred miles to Dublin and a hundred miles behind to the wild Atlantic shore. Often it was Sunday and at Newlands Cross on the outskirts the blues would invariably come calling. Was it a loneliness of evening, of dark coming, a reminder of the brevity of life? A loss of time and place as sure as if he were arriving in to Paris or Los Angeles. In fact he always felt more welcome in those two great cities.

Nowadays you were spared the slow deterioration of the suburban industrial wasteland of the Long Mile Road with its endless motor sales rooms, faux American petrol stations, and nebulous warehouses. You could turn south on the M50 motorway which swept you in a high, curving arc past Rathfarnham and the Hell Fire Club, the pleasant woods of Kilmashogue and eastwards to the sea past Sandyford and Leopardstown to leafier suburban glades. But the city, oh the city. Now neither fish nor fowl. Neither a world-class metropolis nor a homey provincial town. Just a low-rise but endless conurbation that would soon rival Phoenix, Arizona for size and mediocrity. A hundred cranes on the skyline, a thousand new apartment blocks without face or character, symbolized by the minimalist lines of the Spire of Dublin. Signifying nothing. Epicene and passionless. No name, no culture, no country. Old Ireland of his fathers swept away.

And yet his children, born here, didn't seem to feel like this at all. They knew the back streets and the secret places, the tentacles of friends and family that accrue to make a patch of alien earth home. But he, once exiled maybe always would be. Caught between a precarious present and an evanescent past, he never truly could go home again.

He walked into the Tribunal room and there was everything, exactly like he'd left it three months before. The same musty smell, the same dull décor, the same chairs and handrails worn smooth and shiny from a hundred hands and backsides. The same assembled gallery of voyeurs and of course that other well known, often-spotted specimen: the briefless barrister hunting for scraps.

And there was the inevitable, efficient, punctual Martha Williams, immaculate in the harness of her trade: her dark pinstripes, her high-collared blouse, her quills and quiddities. What was it about women professionals? They always seemed more precise and focused, more prepared and trying harder than their male counterparts. And always so eager to please the father figure who sat above them on the bench. Thank God for Cantwell *Fada* and his urbane insouciance. There he was strolling in, calm and collected as ever, always in command. Cantwell reminded Bill of a skilful and reassuring airline captain who always pilots his aircraft through turbulence, landing it in safety no matter what the stormy weather.

Cantwell shook Bill's hand and smiled: 'Good to see you old chap, and I'm happy the headlines have been more favourable to you in recent weeks.'

'Thanks, David,' said Bill, 'but that doesn't earn me any brownie points here I presume.'

'I'm afraid not,' said Cantwell ruefully, 'you've stored up treasure in heaven, but not here on earth. At least not here in Martha Williams's coliseum.'

An apt choice of words, thought Bill. Coliseum indeed. Martha was as fiercely gladiatorial as any ancient Roman but her cool exterior cunningly masked her ruthlessness. He felt pretty sure he had the measure of her since the last encounter, especially the later one in the Morrison. She'd let down her guard to entice him in perhaps, and then slammed the shutters down. And she wasn't catching his eye now he noticed. She was a cold fish without a doubt. Of course she would call it professional *sang froid*.

There she was busily poring over her papers with the winsome-looking Carter in close attendance. He appeared to be shunted to one side, an acolyte running her errands.

'Any idea who Brian Bracken is?' asked Cantwell idly as they waited for the Chairman to arrive.

'Brian Bracken?' asked Bill, his antennae immediately going haywire, as if Cantwell had said the bench they sat on was radioactive. 'Brian Bracken is the manager of my hotel, The Jamesfort.'

'Well, that's her mystery witness.'

'You're not serious,' said Bill. He sat dumbfounded as if struck by a thunderbolt.

'That's the name she sent me last week,' said Cantwell, 'Brian Bracken and another lady called Corinne Daly.'

'Brian Bracken is her witness. My God, he's my right hand man in The Jamesfort. How could she, I mean, is this ethical, can she do this?' Bill had lost his usual calm composure and was temporarily all at sea.

'She can subpoena whoever she likes,' said Cantwell. 'Why? What can he say about you that has you concerned?'

'Nothing...I mean nothing that I'm aware of, but he's supposed to be on my side?'

'Clearly not,' said Cantwell, 'and perhaps that's your clue as to where she came up with her information on your Provo money laundering.'

'But that's all a pack of lies. It's malicious innuendo and nothing else.'

'Well, that's my job,' said Cantwell, 'to establish that. Don't let it worry you. Unless he has proof positive then we'll quickly punch holes in his argument and discredit him. I'm a little bit more concerned with this Corinne Daly. She apparently works in the hotel as well.'

Bill's brow furrowed and he said: 'Corinne Daly? Can't think of who she might be. Probably some new girl employed by Bracken. I do give him pretty much *carte blanche* to hire whom he likes.'

'Maybe that's your weakness,' said Cantwell, 'Not meaning to be critical but maybe you gave this fellow too much rope?'

'I'm beginning to think I did,' said Bill.

At that the Chairman came bustling into the room and climbed the steps to his high eyrie. He smiled good morning to everybody and Counsel for both sides returned the greeting. Brian Bracken slipped in the door at the back at the same time and sat a good thirty feet away from Bill, twelve rows directly behind where he couldn't be seen, because between them were scores of rubbernecking members of the public, cameramen and reporters. A few steps behind Bracken came the svelte and nubile Corinne Daly. She sat beside him.

The Chairman shuffled his papers and then briskly asked the Counsel for the Tribunal if she was ready. She confirmed she was and then called up Brian Bracken. He was dressed in his best grey suit and white shirt and undistinguished tie. The only stand-out accessory was a slim, white handkerchief in his breast pocket which suggested he was spartan, rigorous and clinical. All eyes turned to the tall, mournful man who took the stand and was sworn in. 'You are Brian Bracken, the manager of The Jamesfort Hotel in Kinsale?' asked Martha Williams.

'Yes,' said Bracken, his eyes studiously avoiding Bill Cassidy and his defence team.

'And I believe you have been the manager there for the past five years?'

'Yes.'

'And Mr. Bill Cassidy is the owner of this establishment?'

'Yes he is.'

'Would it be true to say, Mr. Bracken that you have a free hand in running the hotel?'

'Yes, within limits.'

'What are those limits?'

'Mr. Cassidy is given a weekly report of turnover and expenses. He gets bank statements every Monday morning and he's also given a daily report if he requests it. He usually visits once a month for one day.'

'Otherwise you are pretty much in charge of everything?'

'That's correct.'

'So you are aware of all the comings and goings of the hotel and of the approximate income and outlays.'

'Yes.'

'And have you seen anything unusual in the operation of the hotel?'

'Mr. Cassidy keeps a tight rein on any income. Usually the accounts are cleared every week.'

'Can you elaborate?'

'If there are large cash deposits they are immediately cleared from the bank account.'

'And what conclusion do you draw from this?'

'It is unusual. It would appear to be unusual.'

'In what way?'

'It would appear that the money may be used for some... unusual purpose, otherwise why not leave it in the account, earning interest?'

'Do you think Mr. Cassidy is intervening directly to clear these accounts?'

'I can only presume he does it, or else the accountant for the company.'

'You are aware Mr. Bracken that there is an allegation hanging over Mr. Cassidy's head of laundering money for the Provisional IRA?'

'Yes I am.'

'Would this be on all fours with the way the money leaves the accounts abruptly once a week?'

'It would.'

'You say you are given a free hand, Mr. Bracken, does that mean you supervise all the specific income of the hotel?'

'I'm aware of the income, but I don't break it down into profit and loss, Mr. Cassidy's personal accountant does that.'

'I see, so could it be that some of the money going into these accounts is not related to hotel activity?'

'It could easily be.'

'In other words funds could be entered through the accounts from some other nefarious activity but at first glance these funds would appear to be legitimate hotel income.'

'Exactly.'

'What would these funds be labelled as?'

'The accountant could call them miscellaneous accruals, overseas visitor payments, whatever.'

'But you wouldn't know for sure.'

'No because I don't break the numbers down.'

'But you have your suspicions?'

'Yes.'

Martha shuffled her papers, took a furtive look towards Bill and continued: 'Tell me Mr. Bracken, what rating is this hotel?'

'Five star,' said Bracken.

'And I presume it is frequented by five star people, if you follow my meaning?'

'Mostly,' said Bracken, 'but occasionally you can get different types.'

'Such as.'

'People of a slightly more dubious character.'

'How would you know that?'

'I'd get a feeling about it.'

'But you couldn't be certain?'

'Can you give an example?'

'Well, I saw Wild Frank Russell there often with his hangers-on.'

'But he's dead so cannot defend himself here.'

'I suppose not.'

Cantwell jumped up. 'Really Mr. Chairman, Wild Frank Russell was everywhere. I met him many times in the Shelbourne Hotel, at Punchestown, the Curragh.'

'Indeed, so did I,' said the Chairman with a twinkle in his eye. 'Come, come Ms. Williams, are you trying to suggest that Mr. Russell was a dubious character. He made people laugh, got on their nerves occasionally, but I'd scarcely brand him a danger to society.'

'Only with his driving,' said Cantwell to laughter around the room, 'you'll have to do better than that I'm afraid.'

'And scarcely a fan of the Provisionals,' said the Chairman.

'I would have thought the exact opposite, Mr. Chairman,' said Cantwell. 'A sworn enemy more like.'

'Can you name others?' asked Martha rather lamely.

Bracken frowned, racked his brains: 'Not at the moment I'm afraid.'

'Thank you, Mr. Bracken. No further questions for the moment. Please answer any questions which my friend Mr. Cantwell may put to you.'

Bill sat impassively listening to Bracken's speculations. What weasel words he thought. This fellow had some nerve. What game was he trying to play?

Cantwell stood up: 'Mr. Bracken,' he said, 'what earthly proof do you have that Mr. Cassidy is laundering money for the Provos?'

'The money is leaving the account in suspicious circumstances,' said Bracken vaguely.

'You are aware, Mr. Bracken that Mr. Cassidy controls a large network of companies and bank accounts?'

'Yes I am.'

'I mean apart from this hotel?'

'Yes.'

'This hotel represents only a fraction of Mr. Cassidy's entire holdings. No more than maybe ten percent.'

'I'm not sure what the percentage is.'

'Are you familiar with any other bank accounts of Mr. Cassidy's relating to any of his other businesses?'

'No I'm not.'

'Could Mr. Cassidy be merely supporting other businesses that may not be as profitable as The Jamesfort with these cash withdrawals?'

'I suppose he could.'

'But you don't know because you don't see the overall picture.'

'Maybe not.'

'Maybe not? Clearly not! Mr. Bracken, how old are you?'

Bracken looked a little flustered. He looked to Martha Williams. She gave him no succour. 'How old are you sir?' repeated Cantwell.

'Thirty-nine,' said Bracken, sheepishly.

'And what assets do you own?'

'None, apart from my house.'

'Would you like to own The Jamesfort?'

'Would I...' Bracken smiled foolishly, he wasn't expecting this.

'Would you like to own the hotel?' repeated Cantwell.

'I don't see what relevance...'

'Answer the question, would you like to own the hotel?'

'I suppose I would, depending on ...'

'Depending on nothing. You'd like to own this hotel and discredit Mr. Cassidy into the bargain, so after thirty-nine years you might be able to call yourself a minor success in the firmament of Kinsale society?'

Martha Williams was on her feet: 'Really, Mr. Chairman, this is pure speculation. What Mr. Bracken's aspirations or desires are, are of no relevance. He is just a witness here.'

'And a very cunning and manipulative one,' said Cantwell. 'I put it to you, Mr. Bracken that you have cooked up this entire farrago so that you'd like to see Mr. Cassidy indicted and that you could get your grubby hands on his hotel.'

'This is outrageous,' said Williams, turning very red

about the gills and suddenly losing her carefully rehearsed composure. She looked rattled. Bracken looked at her beseechingly like a beaten cur.

There was a pause as Cantwell rustled through his papers. There was a light susurrus of voices from the audience.Cantwell leant over in whispered conversation with Bill and then straightened and said: 'I have no further questions just at the moment.' Bracken heaved a sigh and started to step down: 'But,' continued Cantwell, 'I reserve the right to recall you later depending on what questions Ms.Williams puts to Mr.Cassidy.'

Bill was sworn in and steeled himself to face his by now familiar adversary. No flirting today he noticed. Had she a change of heart or was this merely part of her arsenal? Her bag of tricks. Blowing hot and cold. Trying to unsettle her quarry.

'Do you know where the term money laundering comes from?' Martha asked suddenly, brightly. Bill looked at her with a steady, bemused half-smile.'I couldn't be certain, Ms Williams,' he said dryly.

'Well then, I'll enlighten you.'

'Please do.'

'It comes from the word laundromat, where you wash clothes.'

'Really.'

'Really, Mr. Cassidy. It first appeared in the thirties in Chicago when the likes of Al Capone wanted to clean dirty money which they had extorted from the sale of illicit booze, illegal firearms, the proceeds of drugs, racketeering, race fixing, bank robberies and anything else you care to mention.'

'That's interesting,' said Bill.

'Isn't it just,' replied Martha evenly. 'You see the laundromat business was an all cash business and gangsters literally purchased these legitimate businesses and filtered their ill-gotten gains through as sales, along with legitimate sales. Since nobody was sure exactly how much a whole slew of laundromats might earn there was no way of differentiating the dirty money from the legitimate money. Except it all came out in the wash squeaky clean.'

'Fascinating,' said Bill, 'except where do I come into all this? You're not comparing me to Al Capone are you?' And he gave her his most dazzling smile.

'You're more charming, I'll say that for you but otherwise I see a lot of parallels.'

'Thanks for the compliment,' said Bill with a laugh.

'Oh, that's not a compliment, Mr. Cassidy,' said Martha coldly.

'I didn't think so,' said Bill, 'but I get the impression you watch too many movies. Your imagination is carrying you away.'

'Do you think so?' she asked and her eyes widened in mock innocence. 'But,' she continued, 'the money laundering racket has come a long way from laundromats in Chicago. Nowadays it's much more sophisticated. Transacted with transfers of large amounts of funds to foreign accounts, secret Swiss bank accounts, disguised as large loans, parlayed into overpriced assets and sold onward until it becomes imposssible to tell the original source of the ill-gotten gains. Did you know that one of the easiest ways for Eastern European criminals to legitimise their loot nowadays is to buy a bank? These are easily purchased in places like Estonia, Moldova and so forth. The money goes in hot and comes out as a cold, legitimate loan. The same is done in the hotel business which is where you come in.'

'You're cetainly a mine of financial information,' said Bill, 'but I wonder why if you're so smart you ain't rich, as Al Capone might have said himself?' Loud hollers of laughter rang around the hearing room.

'Come to the point Ms Williams,' said the Chairman impatiently when the laughter subsided. Stung, Martha tightened her lips.'Mr. Cassidy, on the 1st of January last year you transferred nearly ten million Euros into an account in the Chase Bank on Avenue of the Americas in New York, correct?'

'Correct.' said Bill.

'On the 17th of February you transferred a further twelve and a half million Euros to a branch of the Bank of America on Wilshire Boulevard, Beverly Hills, California.' There was an audible gasp from the impressed rubberneckers.

'Indeed,' said Bill.

'Then just a few weeks ago you transferred both of these sums back from dollars into a Euro deposit account with Coutts branch in London. Why?'

'To take advantage of currency fluctuations.'

'How so?'

'In that period of time the Euro rose from approximately 1.18 to 1.28 against the dollar. I made a substantial killing in a short space of time on the foreign exchange market. Over one million.'

'And where did you get this money?'

'Some from an accumulation of cash reserves, some borrowed from a number of Irish and European banks'.

'And none from Provo robberies or cocaine sales?'

'No,' said Bill.

'None from the offloading of hijacked trucks full of cigarettes and whiskey?'

'None' said Bill, 'I'd have used one of those numbered Swiss Bank accounts for that. That way it couldn't be traced.'

Martha folded her arms and nodded, exasperated. 'You are quite the slick operator aren't you Mr. Cassidy, with an answer for everything?'

'If you say so,' said Bill coolly.

'Where did you get the money to buy an office block on 54th Street in Manhattan on the 14th of September two years ago?'

'I borrowed it.'

'All one hundred and eighty million dollars of it?' There was a low whistle from someone at the back. Were their ears deceiving them?

'Yes.'

'And the bank gave you all this money?'

'The bank will give anyone any amount of money provided they have the collateral to back up the loan and the capacity to repay it. That's the way the world works.'

'How easy is it to repay a loan of this amount?'

'It's easier if you get it at interest only for say, five years. That coupled with the rent roll from the enterprise should ensure a smooth passage.'

'A smooth passage indeed. You make it sound easy, Mr. Cassidy.'

'I do my due diligence. I look at maybe a hundred deals before deciding on one. That's the difference between success and failure.'

Martha looked stumped. She nodded trying to size Bill up. She looked impressed in spite of herself. She'd found no chink in his armour. Not yet.

'Are you quite finished?' asked Cantwell with a world-weary smile.

'For the moment,' said Martha coldly, 'but there will be more, I promise you that.'

She sat back down. The Chairman thanked Bill and said he could return to his seat. Cantwell sprang to his feet and said in the light of Mr.Cassidy's evidence he would like to recall Brian Bracken briefly. Bracken strode up with a heavy step and the air of a man not happy with the way the day was going.

Cantwell pulled out a sheaf of papers. He passed copies of them to Martha Williams and copies were handed by a clerk up to the Chairman. Bracken was handed copies. He stared at them and frowned. Cantwell said: 'Do you see the top copy of this sheaf of documents Mr. Bracken?' Bracken mumbled that he did.

'What does it say?' asked Cantwell.

'It says…'

'Read it please.'

' *"Dear Martha, I'm sure Mr. Cassidy is not doing everything above board but I can't exactly prove it yet but I'm working on it. Brian."'*

'Can you read the second one please?' instructed Cantwell.

   ' *"Dear Brian, Would you like to come to the Tribunal to act as a witness against Bill Cassidy? Martha."*'

'Continue please,' said Cantwell, looking around him, enjoying Bracken's discomfort. Bill was looking at Cantwell with a major question mark in his eyes, but Cantwell waved away his query with an, *I'll explain later*, expression.

   'You want me to read more?' asked a pained Bracken. Cantwell nodded. Bracken sighed and blew out his cheeks. His carefully crafted plan was beginning to implode around him.

   '*"Dear Brian, Is there anything specific that you can point to that would actually incriminate Cassidy? Martha."*'

The press gallery was beginning to bubble under. Whispered asides were exchanged behind open palms, scribes were scribbling furiously. Old ladies in the best seats were sitting forward, adjusting their glasses and squaring themselves for fireworks. Po-faced, retired civil servants with their hats carefully perched upon their knees were frowning in puzzlement bordering on dismay. If they'd come to witness a public humiliation they'd come to the right place. Only that of the wrong quarry.

   'Could you read out your reply please?' asked Cantwell, relaxing his deltoid muscles, and cracking his flexed fingers. Bracken looked like he was going to cry.

His voice quivered:

> *"Dear Martha, I'm afraid I haven't anything, but won't the adverse publicity nail him one way or the other…to say someone is sympathetic to the IRA and possibly money laundering is surely very damaging? Yours sincerely, Brian."'*

The gallery was now a rising hubbub of gasps and growls. The Chairman was moved to call for silence. Martha Williams had her face very close to her papers on the desk and wasn't looking up. Bill was sitting back on his pew with an arm stretched out along the back on either side in the manner of a man who has given up trying to figure what the hell was going on. Except it seemed to be going his way for a change.

'And,' shouted Cantwell, now with the concentrated, crouched, pugilistic stance of a man about to administer the *coup-de-grace*, 'can you read out Ms Williams reply?' Ms Williams looked ashen-faced. Bracken squirmed and bit the bullet.

> *"Dear Brian, Bad publicity of itself is not tantamount to a crime but it can certainly cause an erosion of public confidence that eventually might reap rewards, but we have to be careful here. We can't be seen to push the boat out too far. Martha."'*

'Push the boat out indeed. Your words entirely Ms Williams.' Cantwell's words hung like a banner headline in the hushed imagination of the crowded hearing room.

He sat down with a flourish. Martha Williams finally found her voice: 'Mr. Chairman, I must object most strenuously to the introduction of these documents. We were not put on notice that they would be introduced unilaterally without any opportunity afforded us to scrutinize them beforehand.'

'What?' asked the Chairman incredulously, 'are you denying they are an exchange between you and Mr. Bracken? Surely you're not trying to deny that Ms Williams?'

'What I'm saying Mr. Chairman is…'

'Is what? That they're forgeries?' The Chairman looked disappointed and slightly frustrated. Clearly his team had made somewhat of a hash of things.

'No, no but…' began Martha.

'Then what are you saying Ms. Williams?'

'I'm wondering where these copies came from?' faltered Martha.

'I think I can help in that regard, Chairman,' said Cantwell brightly. Martha Williams now looked as bewildered as Bill Cassidy. Cantwell continued: 'I know you have a second witness here to give evidence on your behalf Ms Williams, and may I suggest that it is she who provided the copies of these emails.'

'Who do you mean?' asked Martha, 'do you mean Ms Daly?'

'I do,' said Cantwell evenly.

'But she's a witness for the Tribunal, she's our witness,' said Martha, her entire carefully cultivated image now in tatters. She too looked as if she were about to burst into tears.

'Well perhaps you'd better find out if she is or not,' suggested Cantwell.

There was a hurried confab between Martha and Carter, with furtive looks back to see if Corinne was in the room. Eventually Martha said: 'We have no reason to call this witness, Mr. Chairman.'

'You don't?' asked the Chairman. 'You subpoenaed a witness here today that you're not going to question?' He looked quite annoyed at this point.

'That is correct Chairman,' It was Carter finally talking. His voice was a mere squeak.

'Well, Mr. Cantwell, do you wish to question this witness?'

'Indeed I do, Chairman,' said Cantwell, 'but first I'd like to ask Mr. Bracken one final question before I dismiss him, and it is this. How do you explain the implicit cosiness of your emails with Ms Williams?'

'What are you asking me? ' said Bracken.

'You heard the question,' said Cantwell, 'there appears to be a rather intimate tone in the exchange of emails between yourself and Ms Williams. They don't appear to contain the usual professional distance. Detachment if you will. Correct me if I'm wrong.'

'You're certainly wrong,' said Bracken. 'I don't know how you jump to that conclusion.'

'Mr. Chairman,' shouted Martha her voice now as coarse and angry as a Maggie Thatcher dispatching the opposition, 'Mr. Cantwell is crossing the ethical line here, in making personal insinuations.'

'It may not be me who is crossing that line,' said Cantwell with an unflappable, ironic mien.

'How dare you, Mr. Cantwell!' shouted Martha, Maggie Thatcher personified. The gallery was now in an uproar. The Chairman banged his gavel and said he was adjourning until two in the afternoon. Cantwell said he was happy but would like to call Ms Corinne Daly first thing after lunch and one other witness whose name he would disclose to the Counsel for the Tribunal when she had calmed down and recovered her equilibrium.

Bill and Cantwell went to a small café in Temple Bar that served Italian sausages, tapas and an assortment of breads, baps and dips. Bill had no appetite and settled for a tea and a glass of water. Cantwell allowed himself a glass of white Sauvignon Blanc and a hearty plate of mixed salads. The sunshine crowd were sitting out and the contrast between the relaxed outdoor atmosphere and the claustrophobia of the Tribunal was palpable. Bill was bursting with curiosity about the sudden change in the direction of the examination but Cantwell advised him to be patient. They had come so far and eventual exoneration was sure to follow in the afternoon. They shouldn't jeopardize things now. Bill agreed, his admiration for Cantwell's acumen increasing by the minute.

Cantwell called Corinne up first after lunch. From the recesses of his brain Bill recognized the attractive young lady who had impressed him on one of his visits last year. This was becoming more curious by the minute. Cantwell established that she was an employee of the hotel and asked her had she been summoned here as a witness by the Tribunal. She said she was. He further asked her was it she who had forwarded the disputed emails to him and she confirmed that it was. She further explained how she had come into possession of the emails when asked for assistance by Brian Bracken. Martha Williams fumed at the sudden dilemma she faced of an assumed friendly witness turning hostile.

'Have you by any chance decided to change your evidence here today?' asked Cantwell.

'What do you mean?' asked Corinne

'It would appear that Counsel for the Tribunal think you are now a hostile witness when they supposed you to be a friendly one. They did subpoena you here, correct?'

'Yes they did.'

'And did they ask you beforehand what you were going to say?'

'No, they just assumed I was an assistant to Brian Bracken I suppose, and that I'd back up what he said.'

'But you're not doing that.'

'Certainly not.'

'Another egregious example, Mr. Chairman if I may say so, of the hubris of the Tribunal legal team.'

Martha Williams flayed left and right. She objected to the introduction of the emails once again, she cast aspersions on the intelligence of the attractive blonde in the witness box; but the Chairman dismissed all of her sound and fury. He ruled the emails admissible. Their authenticity was not denied by Mr. Bracken and Ms Daly had a right to voice her concerns as to Mr. Bracken's *bona fides*, based on the content of the emails. The Chairman would make his ruling on what he had heard at the end of the session when Mr. Cantwell had introduced his final witness. The entire room was on tenterhooks in anticipation of who this might be. The crowds, swelled by the gossip machine at full throttle had flocked to hear the dramatic denouement.

'I'd like to call Mr. Joey Harrison,' said Cantwell in stentorian volume as the Chairman finished fixing himself into his seat on the bench above the *hoi polloi*. All eyes turned to a rather battered-looking but well-dressed man walking from the back of the room to take the stand. Joey was calm and collected and back in his natural habitat: expounding for an audience and the bigger the better. Tribunal, High Court or lowly Council Room was all the same to Joey. In fact the higher up the better. Bring them on.

As Joey was being sworn in, Bill looked at Cantwell in disbelief. What was this? What in heaven was Joey Harrison going to say and more importantly which side was he on? With Joey, Bill was never sure. Martha Williams's look of bemusement indicated she had no idea who Joey was or what his presence here could possibly presage.

'You are Mr. Joey Harrison of Reengaroige House, Ardnacarraige, Skibbereen, County, Cork?'

'Indeed sir, I am,' said Joey imperiously.

'And I believe you are a reporter with *The Chronicle* newspaper?' continued Cantwell.

'*Inter alia*,' said Joey with hauteur.

'Of course,' said Cantwell, 'I believe you are also a qualified solicitor, although not presently practising?'

'Correct sir,' said Joey. 'I'm also an amateur historian, literary critic, and bird watcher.'

'And you're a long time acquaintance of Mr. Bill Cassidy?'

'Upwards of forty years,' said Joey, 'in fact I feel I've known him longer than the *Hag of Beara* knew *Fionn McCúmhail*.' His ironic, smiling glance caught Bill's bemused stare for a moment. A titter of laughter went round the assembled gallery. Here at last was a colourful character to shine a ray of sun into the arcane chambers of the law. The Chairman regarded Joey with evident curiosity. 'You're a lawyer you say?'

'Yes, and my father before me. My grandfather was a judge and my great grandfather was shot in the Yukon for his boots, during the gold rush of '98. He took off to make his fortune, leaving a wife and large family behind.'

'And did he find the gold?' The Chairman had a keen sense of humour too.

'Alas that is something we shall never know. But he certainly lost his boots. If he did hit pay dirt none of it ever trickled down as far as myself in County Cork.'

'And why did you never practise law?' asked the Chairman, 'you seem to have a bent for it?'

'I had a granduncle who was a doctor. But he hated blood so he never practised medicine. I have never fancied the fustiness of the law report, nor the tedium of the inconsequential cross-examination. In fact it would appear that the habit of apostasy runs in our family. We consider it an honourable course of action.'

'I see,' said the Chairman, 'intriguing. Carry on Mr. Cantwell.'

Cantwell drew himself up to his full height. He was going to enjoy this. 'Can you tell the Tribunal, Mr. Harrison, in as brief a manner as possible what you have to say concerning the matter before the Tribunal here today?'

'Ah, yes, brevity as Shakespeare says, is the soul of wit, Mr. Cantwell, so I'll try not to crack the wind of the poor phrase by rattling on unduly as you recommend. The point is I've known Cassidy for a very long time and whereas I might not agree with him a lot of the time - in fact a lot of the time I think he's a self-serving son-of-a-bitch, if you'll pardon my French, Chairman - the point is I believe he has been done a grave disservice by the machinations of the witnesses at this Tribunal. After the lurid newspaper headlines pursuant to the last hearing I was dispatched by my editor in *The Chronicle* to investigate. In fairness to my editor he was even-handed and gave me pretty much a free run to see what I could find. Don't get me wrong, Bill Cassidy is certainly highly regarded where we come from but we weren't going to give him a soft ride if the allegations had any substance. But I had a feeling in my waters that these allegations were, and we have a word for it in our part of the world: that word is bullshit.'

The Chairman permitted himself a wintry grin. The stenographer with the bobbed hair and plain face was definitely unimpressed. The gallery fell about laughing. 'So,' continued Joey, playing to the gallery, 'I betook myself to The Jamesfort Hotel in Kinsale to see what I could find. I had a notion from previous discussions with Bill that this place could be his Achilles heel. And I was proved right. I sat, I watched, I waited.'

'And what did you discover?' asked Cantwell.

'I discovered a nest of vipers,' said Joey. 'I always had my suspicions that the source of the rumours about Bill Cassidy laundering money must be coming from within his own camp. Somebody disaffected. This is nearly always the case when somebody falls from grace. Somebody rats on them. I was lucky to meet up with the lovely Ms Corinne Daly who gave evidence here already and we fell to talking about the situation. Before long she let me into her confidence and soon I was privy to the contents of the emails produced earlier.'

'Did you have a hand in influencing her to copy these emails?'

'On the contrary, she'd had the presence of mind to make copies already herself. However I did orchestrate the forwarding of these to yourself and willy-nilly to the Counsel for the Tribunal. Thus it remains and the remainder thus.'

'Indeed,' said Cantwell, 'so you are the unseen hand behind the exposure of Mr. Bracken's dark intent?' Joey permitted himself a modest, affirmative smile. Martha Williams jumped up: 'What is the purpose of bringing this gentlemen here, Mr. Cantwell? Is it to amuse yourself and the gallery here or to waste the Tribunal's time?'

'All will be revealed in a few moments Ms. Williams, when, as Scott Fitzgerald might say, the holocaust will be complete.'

'Well I wish you and your literary genius here would get off the stage,' she said.

'Mr. Harrison have you anything else to say to the Tribunal?' asked Cantwell.

'I have a number of photographs which I would like to exhibit if I may,' said Joey nonchalantly. And he produced from his inside pocket a white envelope which he handed to the Clerk to hand down to Cantwell.

Cantwell took the envelope and extricated a number of photographs, six-by-four inches in size, and he stood gazing at them one by one for approximately one minute. There were ten photographs, produced in triplicate, totalling thirty copies in all. The gallery had gone very still, the Chairman was tapping his pencil on his bench expectantly. Martha Williams had a vacant look in her eye as if she thought the worst was over and was expecting no further humiliations. Bill Cassidy, the subject of the proceedings was sitting back on his hands like a spectator at a circus. Cantwell cleared his throat and said delicately: 'I think Ms Williams you'd better have a look at these.'

'Why,' asked Martha, 'some other cartoon for our diversion?'

'Not quite,' said Cantwell. 'Take a look.'

Cantwell handed the ten top copies across to Martha Williams who took them and sat down very suddenly. She went very pale as she scanned through them one by one. 'Oh, my God,' she gasped audibly. At the same time Cantwell had handed ten copies of the same photographs up to the Chairman. His eyes widened alarmingly as he looked through them. His mouth then hardened into a grim, thin line.

'Do you recognize anybody?' asked Cantwell of Martha.

'Where did you get these?' she hissed to Joey.

'I took them Ms Williams,' said Joey.

'You took photographs of Mr. Bracken and myself?'

'Yes, but not intentionally. I was unable to sleep.'

'You invaded my privacy,' she cried, her voice rising. 'You, you voyeur!'

'On the contrary, Ms Williams, you and Mr. Bracken were embracing in plain sight, and quite passionately if I may say so, like Romeo and Juliet beneath my window,' said Joey. 'You see I was asleep with the fair Ms Daly at my side in my well-appointed suite of rooms in The Jamesfort Hotel. It was the night we had dinner in the Man Friday in Kinsale some months ago. We repaired to the hotel and we retired late after, er...how shall I put it, finishing the evening on a satisfactory note. In the middle of the night, consumed with romantic dreams and unquenchable feelings of emotion in my bosom I sat up in bed gazing at the blithe apparition sleeping beside me. After some moments I idly reached for her mobile phone sitting on the small bedside table beside me and for want of something better to do I started to fiddle with it. To my surprise this device contained an internal camera and the notion struck me to take some pictures of her sleeping, innocent form to preserve the moment for posterity. But then I thought again that perhaps Ms Daly might not approve of my actions although my motives were utterly pure, unimpeachable even. Just as I was vacillating I heard a car pull up in the car park under the window. I heard laughter, some low conversation and then more laughter. Out of curiosity I went to the window, camera phone in hand to see what the commotion was. There below me I beheld to my

astonishment, yourself and Mr. Bracken standing, with
the car door half-open, locked in an embrace of the most
passionate ardour. You were uttering sweet nothings in
his ear and I could see his hands all about you, on your
breasts and on your thighs. I recognized you instantly
because I had seen you both in the Man Friday and I had
recognized you there from previous photographs in the
newspapers, You see you are a very beautiful woman Ms
Williams and instead of recording the lovely, sleeping
Ms Daly for posterity, I was impelled by some force
beyond my control to record your own unforgettable
convulsions in the arms of the debonair Mr. Bracken.'

Joey stopped and waited for Martha to reply. There was
a shocked, stunned silence in the room. A light piece of
paper floated from her desk through motes of dust rising
in the sunlight and revolved slowly like a weightless
satellite in space before settling gently on the floor.
Martha Williams burst into tears and ran in confusion
from the room. Bill Cassidy looked in open-mouthed
amazement at Joey and then at Cantwell *Fada* and then
back to the stony-faced Chairman who suddenly grabbed
his gavel and said quietly: 'Tribunal adjourned forthwith
until further notice.'

As the Chairman stood and bowed to the assembled
legal teams and hurried down the steps and into his
rooms the gallery erupted into mayhem. Flashbulbs
popped and traced the air in huge bright flashes like the
American bombardment of Baghdad, as reporters
climbed over one another to reach Bill, Joey and
Cantwell *Fada*. Old ladies tried to reach Joey, some
brandishing handbags and some wishing to shake his

hand. The straight-laced pillars of society who had come
to see Bill Cassidy hanged, drawn and quartered stood at
the back biting their lips and turning their hats round
and round in their hands as if they were dowsing for
water. The crowd around Bill, Joey, Cantwell and
Corinne grew like a furious, buzzing scrum and gradually
the entire heaving mass of bodies edged in a rolling maul
towards the exit, as harassed policemen shouted to clear
the room. When at last they emerged into the
crepuscular light Bill's ears were buzzing so loudly he had
temporarily lost his hearing. Everything seemed more
colourful, sweeter, warmer, softer, lighter. A great weight
had lifted from his shoulders.

CHAPTER 16

the stars above killiney

Music was all day rising; song and laughter was drifting on the stilly air out over Killiney Bay and south over the Sugarloaf mountain from the midsummer party on Bill Cassidy's wide lawns. It was the longest day and from early morning a continuous line of caterers, gardeners and set decorators had come and gone through the security gates of that mansion on the hill: setting up marquee tents, trimming the borders of hydrangea beds and putting the finishing touches to a party commensurate with Bill's delight at having escaped the clutches of Martha Williams and the Tribunal. Brian Bracken had been dispatched with the withering rebuke of the Chairman ringing in his ears: "pitiable connivances dreamt up and conducted by amateur conspirators in an attempt to destroy a hard-working citizen entitled to his good name." The Chairman would be making recommendations to the Director of Public

Prosecutions to have charges preferred against Bracken and he would also be recommending to the Bar Council to take disciplinary proceedings against Ms Williams for her part in the tawdry affair. Cantwell *Fada* was commended by the Chairman for his stout defense of his client and a fulsome apology was issued to Mr. Cassidy for his suffering and inconvenience. The book was closed on a painful and embarrassing episode and all concerned looked forward to a long vacation and a recharging of their rundown batteries.

It had been wet and dreary in early June but now the dripping fog and sudden, torrential downpours were swept away in the caress of the sultry air that lifted up the hearts of young and old and made their troubles disappear for the time being at least. People were here to party with a vengeance. Out along the manicured lawns and between the pink-flushed flowers of escallonia and towering, spiked delphiniums people moved in ever-changing patterns and groups. Some drifted down by the surging waterfall and sat on the grass as the thundering spray washed over them like a cooling caldarium. Others strolled around the gorgeous beds of dahlias: bright red "Bishop of Llandaff," yellow "Clair De Lune," pink and scarlet "Kathryn's Cupid," shaped like small, exploding suns.

Many, with little or no contact with or acquaintance of Bill Cassidy but whose curiosity was piqued at his recent notoriety, came to drink his champagne and smell the sulphur trailing in his wake. And the rumours flew thick and fast as apple blossoms in a summer gale out over the cliffs of Vico and Shanganagh and drifted like sweet shalimar down to the whispering sea. Because everyone loves a delicious gossip and the more powerful the person with whom it is associated the more thrilling the frisson. The very idea of it. People trying to blackmail a true philanthropic entrepreneur like Bill Cassidy. And the people involved? Not lowly journeymen or women toiling on the fringes, but bulwarks, stanchions even, of middle-class society who should have known better. But there were scoundrels everywhere nowadays: in the Church and in the Law, in all the major professions. Wasn't there a major scandal in the French Government recently when an existing Prime Minister was trying to thwart his rival by investigating a phantom illegal bank account and spreading falsehoods. Shades of that in this case. It was happening everywhere. And then the corollary: was there any smoke without fire? How had he really made his money if not by some dubious means? The questions would remain but to the people breaking out the bubbly on this glorious summer solstice the answer was as inconsequential as the flash of sunlight on a butterfly's wing.

The Hurley-Blacks were here from Foxrock and the Vaughans from Killiney. Catherine Roche, the inveterate socialite, came with someone else's husband, while several well-upholstered divorcées and former models came out in attire so negligible they might as well have come in their birthday suits. Their eyes carried such expressions of alarming and predatory concentration that they were sure to make short shrift of any unsuspecting, available male should he not have his defences stoutly fortified.

David J. Cantwell and his wife, Rosario laughed their way wittily through the velvet afternoon in the company of the society stockbrokers, Peter de Billatrone and his partner Valerie Selway. Cantwell had that slightly eccentric and maverick quality which allowed him to operate on the fringes of show business and racing, and be attracted to dangerously exciting characters like Bill Cassidy. A harmless characteristic which nevertheless might be cause for mild sniffing amongst the benchers and possibly prevent him from getting the nod for a major judicial post by and by. Cantwell didn't care. He was rich as Croesus and peerless at what he did. Besides nothing less than Chief Justice would satisfy his ego.

There was a hardware merchant named John Moore who had made some money (though not as much as he would like people to think he had made) and he was accompanied by his hard-nosed, ambitious wife, who would like to be called a trophy but who was usually referred to as, " old Moore's *Ardmadnac*" after the large quantities of the eponymous duckling she liked to consume in top restaurants in exotic destinations. In a past incarnation, before the liposuction and the collagen she had worked as an announcer on RTE, the national television station, but she quickly became bored with that because journalists didn't make nearly enough money and television producers were essentially penniless factotums masquerading as Hollywood high-flyers.

Also drifting around from room to enormous room was a wrinkly fellow called Jake Breslin who showed up at most society soirées. He was hard to pin down age-wise, anywhere between thirty-five and fifty, and he spoke in a loud, irritating whine. He was given to expounding his ideas on whatever topic that was politically hot at any given time and he used words like "kinetic" a lot: 'The sheer kinetic energy of such and such... blah, blah, blah.' He was something in advertising, probably a copywriter and his current hobby horse was the Provisional IRA and Sinn Fein and the danger of letting them into government. But he was by no means alone in this regard. There were probably another dozen reporters and would-be public saviours floating around clutching glasses of expensive white Bordeaux who suffered from similar paranoia. They mostly sang from the same hymn sheet but liked to studiously avoid each other because competition for listeners was at a premium and these fellows were self-promoting egotists first, last and always.

Thus while Walter O'Flaherty from *The Times* was out holding court in the vast conservatory, Jake Breslin was in the north wing, standing under a Barry Cooke landscape vainly trying to attract the attention of Catherine Roche. Breslin had knocked across the socialite quite a lot in his previous nocturnal peregrinations but his tweedy, intellectual demeanour (apart altogether from the shallow depth of his pockets) wasn't racy enough for Catherine who preferred long-haired rock stars in leather trousers and tattoos on their forearms. She was of the opinion that they had better thrust in the shanks, and Catherine liked to be rogered on a regular basis, no strings attached. There were a few of the species about today, mostly semi-retired, ageing English, glam-rock types who made a bundle in the late eighties but who had long since given up the international gigging to go breeding Group 3 thoroughbreds down in Kildare. But even their legendary sexual energies would now be considerably reduced from too much alcohol, and their olfactory organs in equally dodgy repair from cocaine.

There were a number of politicians on the look-out for votes and quite a lot of *nouveau-riche* property developers including several who flew in and landed on the lawn in brightly-plumaged helicopters. Whenever the opportunity arose, these men-of-the-world would buttonhole the host to ask him if he had anything going this year in Deauville or the Breeders Cup. Bill smiled benignly through it all and while his eyes carried a look of quiet satisfaction at having emerged unscathed from his recent contretemps with the law, they really only sparkled when his two children arrived around seven o'clock as the evening shadows were falling on the lawn.

Barbara, a tall, elegant, dusky brunette, confident and secure in her prime, had flown in from London the previous evening and here she was with her entourage advancing in a royal progress through the house she knew would some day be hers. All eyes turned towards her and an involuntary hush descended on the weary throng, by now exhausted from alcohol and raucous badinage. But here was somebody altogether more formidable than they had laid eyes on yet today and so obviously the apple of her father's eye.

Behind Barbara, with a couple of rugby players from

Clongowes came Daniel, the spitting image of his father,
except even taller at six-foot three, dark and handsome
and causing every girl's heart to flutter. Bill immediately
enveloped his children in a warm embrace and gave an
impromptu speech, welcoming everybody to what he
termed his 'shindig'. He introduced his two children and
then urged everybody to stay as long as they could stand
up in their shoes and to eat and drink to their hearts'
content. Then the family disappeared upstairs where Bill
caught up with the happenings in his children's lives. He
listened to their hopes and fears and he reassured them
that his recent bit of bad karma was now finally behind
him and the future looked rosy. Looking at his two
radiant, fully grown babies, Bill himself realized the
lucky man he was. How strongly reassuring to be
surrounded by the most precious people in his life and on
whose behalf he had been fighting the good fight ever
since they were born. Who knew, maybe their mother
would pay a visit one of these days from the verdant
fields of France.

When they arrived back downstairs and walked out
on the deck overlooking the cascading waterfall, the full
moon of the summer solstice hung like a great orange in
the eastern sky, casting a long, wide, golden road across
the Irish sea. Ships with their lights ablaze moved slowly
up and down the coast and the people around Bill gazed
out upon them and wondered where these ships were
sailing? And the sailors on board those commercial
vessels, homecoming yachts and cruisers, those working
trawlers, looked up at the enormous lit-up mansion on
the hill and wondered what God had come to earth

tonight to take his rouse beneath the stars above Killiney?

At that moment and just as everyone was waiting for Bill Cassidy to reach upward and grasp his beatification from the stars, Joey Harrison arrived all riled up in an advanced state of intoxication. He came from the city in a taxi and leant long and hard on the bell of the security gate, before a butler went running out and led him like a blind horse in by the hand.

'What kind of a goddamn place is this anyway?' Joey muttered looking balefully around him trying to focus. 'You can't get in, and when you're inside you can't get out.' He was progressing to his most truculent and acerbic best and woe betide anyone who crossed swords with him when he was in this mood. He was led in past halls and vestibules treading on squashed orange rinds, strewn flower petals and discarded paper plates until he confronted the drinks cabinet somewhere deep in the bowels of the house and it confronted him. 'What a bewildering choice of beverage,' he said laconically, swaying a little on his feet.

A white-gloved waiter hurried out to Bill on the verandah and whispered in his ear that somebody wanted to see him: an awkward, loquacious fellow who felt Bill owed him something. Bill immediately guessed who his tardy visitor was, behaving true to form as usual. It was more than a week since the Tribunal and Joey had probably spent the time on a drinking binge around the gin mills and watering holes of Dublin. A place he wasn't overly fond of but he liked to get into discussions with the capital's intellectuals, demolishing their vanities with withering logic when well tanked up and eager to demonstrate his superior erudition. Bill, for his part, was still trying to figure out how the collapse of the Tribunal's case came about so precipitately and he was eternally in Joey's debt for that extraordinary scenario. The papers had a field day with the scandal of Martha Williams and Brian Bracken's collusion and Joey Harrison had become a household name. He was hell-bent on exploiting his notoriety and no sooner had word of his arrival at the party been announced than there was a surge of renewed excitement among the jaded revellers.

Bill came in and shook his old friend's hand and Joey stood swaying and wrinkling his nose at him and considered what salvo he was going to direct at Bill to bring him down to earth. Bill, well used to Joey's form, skilfully evaded any confrontation by introducing him to a couple of people who were still managing to hold their liquor at a table in the library. These included Jake Breslin, Jonathan Keel, the filmmaker who was a neighbour of Bill's and whose path had previously crossed with Joey at the infamous UDC meeting some nine months ago. Also present was an attractive, dark-haired literary critic named Amanda Patterson who tended to get breathlessly enthusiastic in the company of anybody famous but who ignored newcomers however talented if they hadn't previously appeared on her radar screen. Joey shook Breslin's hand, noticed the glazed look of dismissal in the literary critic's eyes and chose to ignore her in return. And then when Keel mentioned they had met before Joey looked at him and asked where

could that have been? Joey was no lover of south Dublin
so he must have the wrong man.

'I didn't meet you here, I met you in West Cork last
September,' insisted Keel.

'Never laid eyes on you in my life,' said Joey, and took
a swig of his Scotch which somebody had been foolish
enough to fill for him.

'Well,' said Keel, 'I've laid eyes on *you*, and of course
you have become famous on a number of fronts since
then. The fame is obviously going to your head.'

'And you're obviously still brown-nosing around us
famous people hoping some of the glitter will eventually
rub off on you.'

'Why do you think I'd want to be like you?' asked
Keel. Joey gave a sardonic smile and looked Keel up and
down and said: 'You could never be like me, you'd have
to die and be born again.' The table erupted in laughter
at Joey's witticism. Where had this fellow been all
evening? All year for that matter. The Dublin scene
could do with a character like this. Jake Breslin certainly
seemed to think so. Even Amanda Patterson was
impressed. And so was Catherine Roche who dragged her
leather-clad companion in when she heard that the man
who'd upscuttled the Tribunal had arrived. Word had
also spread that Joey was quite the ladies' man with the
ability to pull blondes like Corinne Daly, and Catherine
was damned if she was going to let such a specimen away
without sampling his attractions for herself.

Before Joey finally took off into the stratosphere he
managed to get a hold of Bill and slurred in his ear that
he had something he should hear that might interest

him. Bill said he'd be happy to hear what this was and Joey said it would require another trip to the south. 'The centre of the universe,' slurred Joey, 'that's where we'll meet, in the centre of the universe.' Bill understood that this was Joey's cryptic shorthand for West Cork and he promised to call him as soon as he had some business tidied up and they'd go out sailing in his yacht. Bill then shook hands with the remaining stragglers who were coherent enough to understand what he was saying and said he was off to bed.

Joey's evening was but a pup. He and Jake Breslin got into an inevitable argument and Joey pointed out to the copywriter that his kinetic movements were annoying him intensely and that he was nothing but a blustering poltroon. The literary critic slowly became more animated as the night wore on and her excited, high-pitched whinnies became louder. They bounced off the high ceilings the more the assembled listeners were reduced to silence, sinking into the waters of alcohol-induced oblivion one by one. One of the last sights to be seen before the sun rose on the bacchanalian excesses of that particular evening was a very inebriated Catherine Roche grappling ineffectually with an incoherent and turbid Joey Harrison in some kind of fumbling, sexual "riverdance." They both finally collapsed in disarray in the immense reception hall, between the fireplace and a side table, sending a long, fluted glass of royal velvet amaryllis crashing to the tiles in a sharded, sodden confusion of exotic greenery and trumpet-shaped red leaves.

The removal men, caterers, gardeners and set decorators came back late on Sunday evening and began

to dismantle the gimcrack paraphernalia of marquee
tents, temporary gazebos and bandstands, and clear up
the wasted, half-consumed provender. They gathered
the detritus of the elaborate display and consigned
everything to the bins of history until Bill decided to put
on another demonstration to the world of all his prowess
and intent. Was he really dealt a good hand by the lord,
born lucky or would that luck run out? Was he
formidable impervious, tough and ruthless? Probably.
And anyone who tangled with him could expect a
bloody nose. Because it was Bill's policy to retaliate
when someone hit him and to continue hitting until one
or other of them was either supine or dead and carried
out on his shield. He hoped he had engendered some of
this iron in his children to carry the Cassidys onward to
the next generation, and this was to be their legacy and
their inheritance. But also the burden on their backs.

The preening gadflies of the social circus had moved on
to the next engagement but to Bill they were as
insignificant as thistledown blown by the restless
summer wind. But those who stood beside him were a
different matter, and apart from his children, these
numbered a small but select few who had soldiered with
him from way back. Some were dead like Wild Frank
Russell and some were living like Cantwell *Fada* and his
absent but steadfast wife, Cassandra. And the
redoubtable Joey Harrison who had arranged a mystery
rendezvous with him on the high seas and which Bill was
anticipating with a curious if puzzled fascination.

CHAPTER 17

the moon at perigree

They sailed out of Baltimore in the early days of
September with portents of autumn in the air. Leaves
were beginning to turn from green to gold. There was a
smell of ripeness and of sweet decay on the northeast
wind. The swallows and the cuckoo had flown south,
and fields of yellow barley were reaching up the slopes
from sea to sky. Bill was at the helm and Joey hopped
around with an unexpected alacrity. Helping with the
rigging: hooking up the halyard and the sheets, and
readying the mainsail for hoisting. He stowed lifejackets
and hampers below and ensured an adequate supply of
beer and victuals for a few days on the ocean wave. They
had the engine running as they were going up the
narrow channel between Sherkin and the mainland.
They passed the Lousy Rocks, Reengaroige Island and
the mouth of the Ilen river. They left Turk Head pier on

their starboard side and continued on down the deep
channel towards Hare Island. Little whirlpools were
forming at this confusion of river and flowing tide and a
sailor had to have his wits about him to avoid the many
barely submerged hazards. They kept the grand manor
house of Whitehall in their sights dead ahead, before
threading through the waterway that separated Hare
Island pier from Cunnamore. And then they were
heading up for the Skeams and out into Roaringwater
Bay. They had no definite objective in mind but to sail
the Atlantic coast west around Mizen Head and
eventually reach landfall at Beare Island on the shores of
Bantry Bay. It was about two hours to high tide on a crisp
and sunny morning. The shipping forecast said the
weather would be mainly fair with winds increasing
later, and a gale warning at 1600 hours, from Mizen
Head to Valentia to Loop Head and up to Bloody
Foreland on the northwest coast. That was not a bother,
they'd be well tied up by then in Castletown
Bearehaven. Maybe just as well. The equinox spring
tides would be higher than usual and coupled with a
southwesterly gale could spell floods and other trouble.

She was a biggish boat, over forty feet and needed a
couple of extra hands if they were to go farther. But with
the weather fine and no hurry the two of them should
manage well enough. Besides Joey seemed keen that
they should go alone and Bill was happy to oblige. But
Bill wondered why the secrecy? Joey was on his best
behaviour, stone sober if maybe a little uptight. Perhaps
it had to do with whatever was on his mind. With Joey
you never could tell exactly what was coming next.

Except it was certain to be interesting. There he was, well buttoned up in his sailor's sweater, Aran fisherman's trousers tied with a colourful *crios,* soft, brown pampooties on his feet and sailor's cap, the entire ensemble securely fastened under a red and white life jacket. Bill himself was caparisoned in more conventional attire: polo shirt and sweater, shorts and deck shoes without socks, shades perched on his head above his forehead.

Joey was all action. One minute he was for'ard in the bow checking a shackle or attaching a forestay to the bowsprit. The next minute he was back in the cockpit looking astern to ensure the rudder was free of seaweed or other flotsam. He certainly knew his sailing, Bill would grant him that. He knew these waters far better than himself. In his youth Bill had been a landlubber, but Joey's crowd were always well-heeled enough to own a boat. How things had changed.

There were few other boats about. Although still only early September the summer yachtsmen had all gone back to the cities, mooring their craft in Schull or Baltimore or Crookhaven, leaving the vast ocean to the hardy few or those who depended on it for a living such as the ferries and the shell fishermen. You had to keep a sharp eye out for the ferrymen. They came at you at a rate of knots, ploughing through treacherous, deep trenches with jagged rocks rearing up on either side and woe betide any small craft in their path. There was the Cape Clear ferry now, just astern, gone down between Hare Island and ridges of rocks in a channel that Bill thought was too narrow for his own boat. But these swashbucklers always took the shortcut, regarding all pleasure craft as nuisances to be frightened off or overturned if they strayed too close. Some smaller lobster and mussel boats were out as well. They chugged in and out of inlets and shallow bays with hardy fishermen in sou'westers and yellow leggings and cloth caps standing up nonchalantly in the stern, working their deliberate way over the crystal blue-green water, with nothing for company but lazy seals, shags and herring gulls.

Away up the bay, past the parallel lines of fish-farming nets held up by floating, plastic barrels, Kilcoe Castle stood out like a brilliant cheese-coloured beacon against the blue water and the green shore. A surefire landmark for tired and weary mariners returning on a pale, misty twilight from harvesting the shoals of herring.

They cut off the motor between the western Skeam and Hare Island and hoisted up the mainsail. Then they ran the jib up. The wind was coming from the landward side, directly at their back straight over Kilcoe and Ardura Beg. It was a light, cool breeze causing only minor ruffles on the water but it had strengthened a little since they cast off. They should get a good run before it now, and with the tide soon turning the sailing should be smooth and easy down past the Calf Islands to starboard and Cape Clear to port, out towards the Fastnet. 'Do you think we should let up the spinnaker?' shouted Bill, 'while we have a fair wind behind us?' Joey was standing amidships with one foot on the starboard gunwale, loosening the jib sheet. 'Let me let the jib out a little more,' he said, 'then we'll set her.' Joey made some minor adjustments and then ran the spinnaker up. She blossomed out and billowed like a beautiful balloon: blue and yellow and scarlet red. The boat shot forward visibly and smacked off the rising waves. The sky was not quite clear, southwest there were darker cumulus and westward reared the pyramid of Mizen Peak. Joey came and sat alee, while Bill still stood athwart and screwed his eyes on the horizon as the wind sang in the sails. Joey broke out two cans of beer and they slaked their thirst. He was in ebullient mood:

> *"Push off and sitting well in order*
> *Smite the sounding furrows."*

'Do you know that one? Ulysses by Tennyson.'
'Vaguely,' said Bill, 'carry on.'

> *"For my purpose holds to sail*
> *Beyond the sunset and the baths*
> *Of all the western stars until I die.*
> *It may be that the gulfs will wash us down*
> *It may be we shall touch the Happy Isles*
> *And see the great Achilles whom we knew..."'*

'You're a poet and you don't know it,' said Bill.

'This is the life,' said Joey. He could sit back now and relax awhile. Their course was set. The salt of the spray and the tang of sea was something he'd neither tasted nor smelt for many a year. And the huge silence; except for the flapping of the sails, the wind singing, the sucking, eructating water and the creaking of the spars and stays. It took him back to happier days, young and easy in the fountain of his youth. He shifted his backside on the after transom. These new boats were luxurious to a fault. Everything smooth and soft. He'd become soft himself. He looked slyly at his old buddy and noticed the erosion of the years around his eyes and hair. But not that much. This guy was holding up well. A tough one right enough. Would he be tough enough to withstand the news Joey had enfolded in his inside pocket? He had to hear it sooner or later and hopefully it would eventually raise his spirits up, though shake him to his roots at first.

Joey finished his can of beer. So did Bill. Joey cracked open two more and they flew towards the mighty Fastnet Rock where they might spot some whales who had come last month in the pale light of August.

Three hours later they were southwest of the Fastnet. They saw two whales blowing spouts of iodine-suffused water high in the air. Joey said they were finbacks but Bill said no, they were humpbacks or maybe sperm whales. 'Finbacks I tell you,' said Joey, 'the spouts are too high for humpbacks and the sperm whale has a larger tail fluke and an angled spout.' Bill conceded. The man was a walking encyclopedia.

And then a school of jumping dolphins passed them smiling. They saw guillemots and razorbills and Manx shearwaters. And flocks of storm petrels hurtling low. They saw ospreys with pale under-parts and narrow, fingered wings, plunging, talons-first into the sea for fish. In their exhilaration they noticed neither time nor weather, nor the distance they had sailed. They were gently soused from numerous cans of beer and the rocking of the waves made them a little drowsy. The tide was ebbing now, swinging them further out and with the sails all standing they were well away from shore. There was a build-up of cloud and the wind was wheeling around to the northwest. There were clouds of puffy cumulus pushing south. Some were white like sheep's wool and some were darker, brimstone-blue. Underneath were red-ribbed mackerel clouds blown eastward, and in between were wisps of angry grey. It was already four o'clock and the angle of the sun had changed: gone west and down the early autumn sky. They were like lotus eaters drunk on life's sweet, simple pleasures. And Joey spake:

> '"Let us alone time driveth onward fast
> And in a little while our lips are dumb
> What is it that will last?"'

'You're some fatalist,' said Bill, feeling his burnt brow. The rudder was on autopilot; no hands on the wheel. Bill sat abaft on the starboard side.

'Do you believe in miracles?' asked Joey, his voice changed from its earlier clarity to a throaty slur.

'No,' said Bill, 'a man controls his own life.'

'Do you believe in coincidences?' continued Joey. He could transfix even the most independent-willed with a stare in this mood.

'I see coincidences all the time,' said Bill, 'but they can be explained mathematically.'

'Like hell they can,' said Joey. 'On the contrary, it's all preordained. There is such a thing as destiny. There is a God you know.'

'If you say so,' said Bill and examined a winch beside him.

'Cynicism doesn't become you,' said Joey. 'You think you've covered all the bases. Thought of everything. Dispatched everybody.'

'As much as possible,' said Bill evenly. His friend was getting quite exercised. Better try to soothe him. Joey paused and looked behind at their furrowing wake and then looked back at Bill: 'What if I told you that you had a son, a grown man?'

'I have a son,' laughed Bill, 'and he is a grown man, more or less.'

'I mean another, older son.'

'Another son?'

'Another son, named George Conklin.'

'George Conklin?'

'Yes, the young American, the one I had burnt out.'

'You burnt him…? Well, I always figured that. But how the hell is he *my* son?'

'He's Eileen's son. Remember Eileen McManus? And your son.'

Bill turned visibly pale under his tan. He stared at Joey but didn't see him. He was looking back over thirty years. He was counting. He stood up and took hold of the helm wheel. The boat dipped and rolled through a trough and rose on the crest of a wave. A strong swell was rising. They had already hauled down the spinnaker. Bill reached over automatically and slackened the jib and mainsail sheets: 'How do you know this?' he asked, like a man in a dream. Joey silently produced a neatly folded letter from his trouser pocket. 'Read that,' he said.

Bill took the letter. Joey saw his hands were trembling. He sat down again and read to himself:

"*Dear Mr. Harrison,*
After I spoke on the phone to George and yourself I did some research as you requested. I had to scour around some but eventually the Hall of Records in Santa Monica provided the answer. I had to call in a favor or two from some old friends in the Municipality but anyway here's what I found. An Eileen McManus is listed as being the mother of a baby boy named George born on the 22nd of October 1975 in the Santa Monica General Hospital. The father is named as a William Cassidy. Both parents are listed as being from Cork, Ireland. The baby was adopted by a Samuel (that's me) and Virginia Conklin.

I hope this information will help Georgie to find what he's looking for.

All the best,

Sam Conklin."

Bill continued to stare at the letter. He reread it several times. The slackened sails flapped, the spray flew in the rising wind. Bill's expression to Joey was a pained, beseeching question. Joey said: 'Remember the day you left her in the desert? Left us I should say. Remember? I stayed with her. You were gone. Well, she was already a month pregnant at that stage and she didn't know it. She was worried about something. Anyway you were long gone and, as they say, hard to find. Oh, we tried various methods of contacting you: addresses of other friends and some cousins of yours in Boston, but Christ knows where you were.'

Bill nodded ruefully: 'I went east as far as Tennessee and the Blue Ridge Mountains. Then I went west again on a Greyhound Bus through Indiana, Illinois and Wyoming. I travelled all over, eventually ending up in Boston, then New York.' Bill was talking for the sake of talking. Inside he was rattled to the core.

'Well in all that time,' continued Joey, 'she was getting bigger and bigger and more anxious. I had to stay with her. Eventually she quit her job in that fish restaurant in Venice and we managed to scrape the funds for the hospital. It was a difficult birth, but she didn't want me there. In fact I never even saw the baby. She always said she was going to have it adopted and that is what she did. Mind you it broke her heart. She didn't want me around after that. It was some kind of catharsis for her, if that's the word. Or trauma or whatever.'

Bill stood up again and went through the mechanical motions of a man whose mind was elsewhere. He turned on the radio. There was a gale warning in operation. It was a disembodied voice from the coastguard.

'Attention all shipping. Northwesterly winds will reach gale force this evening and tonight. Winds will reach gale force eight or nine and possibly storm force ten.' The radio crackled out. They had just tuned in to the tail-end of the message. Bill clicked it off. 'Better turn about,' he said, 'standby.' He slackened the sheets of the mainsail, winching them out. 'Ready about,' he said. Joey nodded but his body moved slower than his mind. Bill swung the wheel. Joey ducked and slouched across, barely missing the swinging boom. The slack sail flapped wildly. 'Pull on that,' shouted Bill, 'quick, the winch.' Joey managed to secure the winch on the port side and they were going into the wind. 'Any idea where we are?' asked Bill.

'Somewhere south of Brow Head,' said Joey. 'We should probably head back for Crookhaven.' The sky had darkened visibly. There was a massive cloud, an indigo monster, blue-black in parts louring out of the west. It had swallowed up the sun. It was cold, with rain impending. Bill's heart was heavy. 'Why didn't you tell me all this before?' he asked of Joey. Joey made a blowing sound with his mouth like a Frenchman and shrugged: 'Because I had no proof I suppose. No definite proof. A lot of reasons.'

'Didn't she tell you I was the father?' asked Bill. Joey was evasive. 'She was very secretive. You broke her heart you know. Then giving away the baby broke it a second time. She soldiered on for four or five years when she came back home. But she didn't want to talk to me. You were the one she was waiting for and you never came. Sorrow killed her in the end. Sorrow and sadness and regret.'

'But I saw you at her funeral, you could have told me then,' said Bill.

'It was too late by then,' said Joey. 'What was I supposed to do? Add to your misery.'

'I can't believe that I never knew. That all those years I never knew.'

Bill looked up at the darkening heavens as if expecting some comfort from the elements. 'All those years, all that time.'

'Over the years you kind of forget,' said Joey. 'After awhile it is real no longer. You erase it from your memory. You should know that.'

'How should I know? asked Bill.

'My dear Bill you have an excellent facility for amnesia,' said Joey wearily. 'You forgot your father, you forgot Eileen and you'd have forgotten me except I had a habit of showing up like a bad penny every now and again. But I've no doubt you could have lived without me easily as well.'

'So that's why you wanted to come out here,' said Bill a little bitterly, 'to remind me of my failures?'

'Let's just call them derogations,' said Joey, 'or obliquities.' Bill smiled grimly. The wind was louder, stronger now and the waves were higher. They thrashed against the prow, sideways-on, making headway difficult with the tide still not turned. They painstakingly tacked their way back the way they came, beating north by northeast. Visibility was now well down and a cold rain was falling. Joey tried to put on a cheerful demeanour, although quite drunk by now. He faltered:

'"*This mounting wave will roll us shoreward soon.*"'

Bill realized he might have to do this on his own. 'We'd better keep our wits about us out here. Why did you have to bring me out here to tell me all this anyway?'

'You've been running all your life, Billy boy,' said Joey, almost triumphantly, 'but there's no running away out here, eh?'

'So who do you think you are now, the divine

redeemer passing judgement on us all?' asked Bill scornfully.

'You think there's no retribution?' shouted Joey. His eyes were blazing. 'You think you can ride rough-shod over everyone in your path and pay no price? Avoid consequences and suffering? Postpone the evil day? Well, everyone pays a price.'

'This is no time to be educating me,' said Bill sourly. The wind was taking his breath away. They toppled into a deep trough and climbed up the other side. From the crest they could just make out the Fastnet to leeward. 'It's getting late,' said Bill. 'It must be after seven. How far out are we from shore do you think, an hour?'

'Two hours,' said Joey.

'We've misjudged this badly,' said Bill.

'What of it?' said Joey nonchalantly, 'what will be will be.' Bill was becoming irritated. Did this man have a death wish? Probably. Damned if his moroseness was going to affect Bill. He said so.

'It's out of our hands,' said Joey, 'the moon is at *perigree.*'

'What's that?' asked Bill.

'It means the *declination* of the moon's orbit is at minimum.'

'So?,' said Bill.

'So the tides are higher than usual. It's a coincidence that happens only every twenty years. The sun, moon and earth are lined up in a straight line. This makes the gravitational pull on the oceans stronger. We have no control over it. It's an astronomical phenomenon. You think we control our destinies? My dear man we are like mere flies, welter to the Gods of physics. It's a time of eclipses, curses, prophecies coming to pass.'

Bill sighed. He steered the conversation back to what he could control.

'What's this about burning George out anyway, as we're on the subject?' he asked.

'I made it happen,' said Joey. He sounded proud. 'I didn't do it but I made it happen. I got a few wide boys for Keohane. Keohane and some wide boys did it.'

'Keohane the publican you mean?'

'The same man,' said Joey. 'We had our motives of course, but I'm sorry now, too late. Now that I know who the boy is. That's why I've tried to make reparation, why I've confessed my sins. But I too must pay a price. The Gods are vengeful.'

'I notice you didn't confess your sins to the police,' said Bill caustically.

'No more than you confessed yours to the Tribunal,' retorted Joey, 'I saved your ass there for sure, but if I hadn't done so you'd have found someone else to do it. You'd go through the eye of a needle here on earth, Bill Cassidy, but not in heaven. Heaven knows of your corruptions. They go back a long way but of course nobody can now prove them. Just like me and the burning thatch. And you are too rich and powerful. But back in the early days is where it all began. First you cheated your own father and then the beautiful Eileen. Then you continued in a hundred deals and venalities and manipulations. Nobody becomes as rich as you without doing it this way. You are not alone. But don't pretend to dress it all up in the end as the triumph of capitalism and our democratic way of life. You are corrupt Bill, corrupt and venal to the core. You and all your ilk. You couldn't hold your father's coat!'

Joey was roaring and his tirade rose above the howling wind. The rain was coming down in streams, splattering concentric circles on the water. How far now to shore? Dimly ahead the wide bay of Toormore was opening its arms. They were driven eastwards from Crookhaven despite their efforts to go in. Back towards Castle Point they were blown by huge, high-rolling breakers. Bill tried to hold the boat steady and Joey was spent in miserable exhaustion on the cockpit floor, like a penitent at prayer; sidereal speculations abandoned. From behind, a huge, high rogue wave towered like a tsunami above them. Bill saw it too late. Joey turned his eyes towards it and crossed himself.

'The vengeance of the Lord,' he cried as the wave broke over them with shattering power. It smashed the jib away from the mast and the mainsail flapped in tatters. The mast was fractured, if not quite broken but how long could it last. The wind was a howling banshee. There were rocks up ahead and the shore close, but first this treacherous reef. All along it's petrified, jagged back, cormorants, shags and fulmars sat and watched like waiting spectres; lifting their wings and cronking, and swivelling their wild and glittering eyes. 'Standby to tack,' roared Bill. Joey lurched awkwardly to his feet, sodden and dripping. 'Lee-o,' shouted Bill, spinning the wheel. 'Let go the jib sheet, let it go.' Joey was slow to follow his command. The boom came round and caught Joey with a sickening crunch on the head and he went over the side like a flipped fender into the churning surf. Bill threw the stern line to him as he thrashed about, gasping, going under and coming up; his arms like wild and incoherent semaphores flailing for the line. With his other hand Bill hauled desperately on the winch but the mast had lost its purchase. The sails flapped like broken umbrellas without use or purpose. The boat inched along the reef, as breaker after curling breaker cascaded over it. There was a tearing and a grinding as the port bow hit the reef, opening a gaping wound below the water line. Bowsprit, halyard, spars, and cleats cracked and flew. The mast came down with the mainsail and the headsail, enveloping Bill like a ragged shroud.

Joey was dreaming of the burnished California coast. The view up past Pacific Palisades towards Malibu was hazy-blue, and beckoning. He was walking at morning along the wide, peaceful shore and as the sun's rays burnt off the coastal fog the beautiful, white pier appeared as a mirage in the glassy light. And there was Alice's Restaurant sitting at the end. The coast unfolded before his eyes like wrinkles of a great cloak. He passed Goleta, Santa Barbara and he flew over San Simeon by the sea. He looked and said I'm staying here forever. And he wondered why he was so hard on his old friend Bill when he himself had still kept something back? A man is always less than frank in the heel of the hunt. And why did he not say to him: 'But Bill, I loved her too. I loved her too when you had gone.'

Bill was falling, falling and thinking, how pleasant to be

falling. No lawyers and no bank accounts, no mortgages. No profits and no losses. And what was patrimony and what was primogeniture and other crazy phrases? And he saw his children's faces and he saw George's face. Was he really all that like him? Never stopped to think because not knowing. Until he saw Eileen standing on the cliff face, smiling. She reached out for him and as she folded him in her arms he knew his search was over. And he was young and free without a shilling, but what of that. It was a warm September evening. He had a lovely girl by his side. The harvest moon was moving up the sky. Shandon's bells were ringing and a jazz band played in town. From somewhere in the gloaming two saxophones were blowing on the blue September wind. And they lay down to sleep together beyond the moon at *perigree* and very far away. Much further than Carberey's Hundred Islands and the lonely Roaringwater Bay.

CHAPTER 18

icarus children

They found Joey's body quite early the next day in a misty lagoon where the water slapped against the rocks. The fury of the waves had long since abated. He had a kind of peaceful smile on his face as if he'd welcomed death and was happy to cross over to the fatal shore. It was a local fisherman who found him as he hunted for shellfish and crabs among the rocks. First he came across the jetsam of the vanquished boat and then he saw the body. He raised the alarm and soon the Baltimore lifeboat was on its way to gather Joey in and take him home.

It was nearly twenty-four hours later when they found Bill Cassidy many miles to the west around the Mizen. The lifeboat men reckoned he must have put up a mighty battle to survive. Soon after, the doctor who examined him confirmed their opinion. He said he wasn't dead very long. Maybe two hours. The lifeboat men estimated the boat foundered around seven o'clock in the evening. When they found his body it was around seven o'clock the following evening. He must have fought heroically against those tremendous waves.

They took the bodies into Baltimore and later into the mortuary of the University Hospital in Cork where a post mortem was held. Death by accidental drowning was the verdict. Bill's wife and children were very quickly made aware of the tragedy and came to Cork in shock to bid their father a final farewell. And George Conklin simultaneously put two and two together and discovered too late who his father was. And his mother too. His uncle Sam Conklin contacted him and sent him a copy of the letter he had sent to Joey. The letter which had come as a body blow to Bill. And George could only reflect sadly that the man who had abandoned him even before he was born had by a strange turn of destiny also saved his life from the inferno and then lost his own life to the sea.

Bill's enormous mansion stood empty like a mausoleum except for the gardener who continued to keep the grass mown, the hedges trimmed, and the aspidistras watered. There was a shuddering in the interlocking systems and companies he had created. They slowed to a standstill for a number of days before accelerating back to their usual smooth runnings. Impervious to Bill.

Joey's funeral was held first and he was buried in the graveyard beside his parents within sight of the rambling mansion where he spent his days plotting subterfuge and launching broadsides against foes real and imaginary. And what had made him stand by Bill yet fight him to the end? Was it the promise and the thrill of being an Icarus child when he flew with his old friend? And what had caused the spiral fall? Was it because the speed brought them too close and the intensity burnt their hopes like charred feathers?

They laid him down beside his father and his mother, proud people, sure of their worth, solid and secure in their time and place, loyal friends, fierce in battle. And the wide Ilen that he loved so well would run on past his gravestone unaware of the formidable, unsentimental figure who slept besides its banks. He was at peace at last, no longer needing to be alert, acerbic, vigilant. Someone else would have to take up the cudgels now. And carry the baton.

The crowds who came out to bury Bill Cassidy were not as great as might have been anticipated. For sure some of the great and the good showed their faces: captains of industry, politicians, soldiers and sailors, gamblers and horsemen. Neighbours who knew him from his early years. Old friends of his parents. But all in all surprisingly few. There still remained a large deficiency and the outpouring of expected grief did not materialize. People went through the perfunctory motions, did their duty by him, but no more. Was it because the *zeitgeist* sensed something hollow in his ultimate attainments, some ephemeral penumbra of an inconsequential grandeur he was chasing which was not worthy of his true potential?

Cantwell *Fada* gave a graveside oration and spoke of

the first time he had met Bill Cassidy and what had drawn him to him. Of his talent and accomplishments there was no doubt. Neither of his generosity or of his courage and tenacity. But what was it he was chasing? What drove his restless, peripatetic spirit? Perhaps Bill was never sure, perhaps never really knew himself. Buffeted by conflicting energies, made vulnerable by early loss and the pains of deprivation. That he flew close to the sun there was no doubt. Neither was there any doubt but that he left his family well set up and that his long-lost son George would at last be welcomed into the bosom of a wider clan. His story was the story of a modern Ireland, when the sun was setting on a bruised and battered twentieth century and facing the rising sun of the twenty first. He came from a generation unshackled by the burdens of the past; a generation free to dream? Joey had said he betrayed his father, but surely Bill's success is what his father wished for, fought for even. So that Bill could conquer the world. So what was Bill to do? Carry on, stand on previous giant's shoulders, become a giant himself. But was Bill's story as grand as his father's story? And had his essential self-conceit blinded him to his shabby treatment of that heroic man. And of the loyal, beautiful Eileen. He fought off his enemies and kept running to the end, the future receding ever faster and every time his reach exceeding his grasp. But could he fill his father's shoes as Joey said, or hold his noble coat? Or was he forever blinded by the lure of a pervasive and materialistic avarice which held him in its sway. That he might have emerged unscathed from the Tribunal was not the ultimate point. People weren't fooled by his sleight of hand and were perhaps disappointed that somewhere back along the winding roads of life he had taken a wrong turn and in his haste had gone astray.

Cantwell finished his oration at Bill's grave. He was buried in the foothills beside his parents and not far from Eileen's grave, looking west towards the thunderous Cahas; the first range his boyhood eyes beheld and that would always be the *Great Divide* he had to cross to find the new frontier. His children, Barbara, Daniel and George held hands and looked towards the sunset. It was Autumn now. The fruit was ripe in orchards. The evening was still and crystal clear. The wheatfields in the distance shone like prairies of gold.